Praise fo
# Be Hopeful, Be Stron
# Curious: How Coaching Can Help You Get Out of Your Own Way and Create a Meaningful Life

T0293597

"This book is both a compass and a map to a new version of you. Buy this book, read this book, and step into something bigger!"
*—Tim Jaques, Founder and CEO •*
*Teaming Worldwide*

"Ruth is a MACHINE! I am in awe of how quickly she wrote this book. And, of course, it's AMAZING. The chapter titles and sequence are perfect, and I really like how she's included so many voices. In fact, my jaw dropped when I saw echoes of our conversation around meaning in the first chapter! That was so cool, I really like what it's become."
*—Kari Kelly, Enterprise Agile Coach at*
*Dandy People*

"Ruth Pearce is an exceptional writer and storyteller. In this book, Ruth explains how and why coaching works. The book is written with positivity and hope, clearly stating what coaching can do for you. Ruth is both strong and brave in sharing vulnerability about her own successes and failures—and throughout the book she remains curious about why."

"The case studies are a wonderful opportunity for Ruth to showcase exactly how coaching works in a way that resonates with the reader. Ruth also includes coaching questions and various points in the book for self-reflection and self-coaching. These value-added features make the book both practical and accessible for anyone who is considering hiring a coach for their development. As a coach who often finds it challenging to explain what coaching is, I am looking forward to referring potential coaching clients to Ruth's book for guidance on whether coaching is right for them."
*—Asila Calhoun, ACC, CIC, PHR, SHRM-CP,*
*Principal & Leadership Coach*

"This book feels like a powerful self-audit. It is meant for individuals who are considering coaching, and yet it is very helpful for coaches too. Reading it as a coach, it challenges you to think, what must I dial up? What must I dial down? What questions would I have asked? Is this question more powerful—do I want to add it to my toolkit? So if you are a coach with limited opportunity to hear from other coaches, this is a really good book."

*—Irene Poku, UN Women UK Delegate to the*
*UN CSW67 | Authentic Leadership Coach*

"Learn from the best positive psychology coach there is—this book will show you how to be curious about your strengths and resources, how hope can make you discover the opportunities that are before you, and how you can utilise bravery to follow your plan and make the decisions that will lead you to your better future!"

*—Marjorie Aunos, PhD, Psychologist, Speaker,*
*and Accessibility Consultant*

"With this incredible new book, I now have Ruth's coaching advice at my fingertips. It's a must-read for anyone hungry for guidance. She is incredibly insightful, deeply committed, and passionate about unlocking her clients' true potential."

*—Clarissa Schuh, High Tech Sales Enablement Manager*

"Ruth has the unique ability to challenge us with profound questions and encourage us to face the future with active hope and bravery. In her new book, she demystifies the coaching process, offering valuable insights on how to overcome obstacles in the life journey toward finding purpose and meaning."

*—Renata Rangel, MSc, Career & Well-Being Coach*

# Be Hopeful, Be Strong, Be Brave, Be Curious

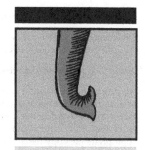

# Be Hopeful, Be Strong, Be Brave, Be Curious

How Coaching Can Help You Get Out
of Your Own Way and Create a
Meaningful Life

Ruth S. Pearce

WILEY

*This book is dedicated to YOU!*

# Contents at a Glance

# Contents

# Foreword

by Dana Brownlee

It's not enough to have strengths and talents. We all have them, but too often we can't necessarily see them as others do—just as we can't see the nose on our face.

During my early years as a corporate trainer, I'd worked hard to catch the attention of a major international training organization. Having launched my own company after a decade or so of traditional corporate experience, I was more than confident about my abilities facilitating dynamic and engaging sessions, but securing the clients was not just a challenge but downright terrifying at times. That's why the opportunity to partner with a leading international training company was beyond enticing. While I was thrilled to talk to them about coming on board as a contract trainer, I felt a gut punch as the instructor relations representative explained that they were interested in bringing me on not to teach the team building courses I'd grown comfortable executing but instead to teach a project management requirements course—ouch! While I immediately pushed back on that, insisting that "requirements management" wasn't my sweet spot (while internally nursing feelings of inadequacy and terror), she, undeterred, methodically walked me through my own résumé, pointing out my broad range of experience, specifically that of eliciting, documenting, and managing requirements on an array of technical projects over several years. The more we chatted, the more I could see my own expertise, which I hadn't just minimized but completely ignored.

I trusted her assessment, began teaching that course, and absolutely thrived. My students over the years gave me rave reviews in particular because I was able to weave in so many tangible, practical examples from my years of management consulting experience. A few years later, having taught multiple course titles successfully, I was asked by the same training company to author a new Business Analysis course, their flagship course for the new topic area. Again, I was hesitant, uncertain, and resistant, but their representative again talked me through how my corporate experiences were a strong fit for the course content, and, in doing so, they bolstered my confidence around growing into the prominent leadership role of course author. Within months of our conversation, I'd not only authored a newly successful course but also traveled around the United States and beyond, teaching inaugural course events that other instructors could audit to prepare them to teach the course as well. I wasn't just the lead instructor but also the leading authority guiding instructors, making content decisions and influencing the direction of the course. I'd grown into a much broader, more influential role, and they'd coached me through that process. While I'd garnered the raw talent years earlier, it was their periodic coaching, which I had no idea I needed, that helped me begin to see the breadth and depth of my talents for the first time.

That shift changed the trajectory of my business, my career, and, ultimately, my sense of self. That type of support and enlightenment is a gift that we all deserve to have as we work to create our most fulfilling and impactful lives. That's why this book is so critically necessary. It's a guidebook to help each of us self-reflect and determine whether coaching can become a pathway to achieving new levels of performance, accomplishment, and personal contentment.

If you have ever thought about dipping your toe into the "coaching waters," this book is for you. Ironically, those who haven't seriously thought about it might benefit even more. In *Be Hopeful, Be Strong, Be Brave, Be Curious*, coaching guru Ruth Pearce uses a mindful, strengths-focused approach to demystify a concept that's often misunderstood: the world of professional coaching.

The world is full of critics—people to point out your faults and gaffes—but Ruth's brilliance, as a mindfulness practitioner and coacher of coaches, is her passion around helping others identify, celebrate, and leverage their unique strengths. A longtime VIA Character Strengths facilitator, Ruth's top strengths are Appreciation of Beauty & Excellence, Bravery,

Curiosity, Fairness, Gratitude, and Hope, and those are the traits and values that undergird each chapter as she outlines a roadmap for you to take a personal inventory of your own readiness to explore coaching as a resource for enhanced growth and development.

The truth is that when our strengths are ensconced within our blind spots, we're tapping into only a portion of our potential. Tragically, it's the strengths that are most inherent in our personality, the most automatic, that can also be the most unconscious and unrecognized. We more likely just assume everyone is wired that way and miss the uniqueness of our talent.

Unfortunately, unrecognized talent can translate into missed opportunity year after year after year.

If you're wondering whether you're really tapping into your full potential or perhaps missing valuable growth and achievement opportunities, consider these questions that the book helps you explore:

What is coaching anyway?

What myths have you internalized about who gets coaching and why?

Are you a good candidate for professional coaching?

Are you ready to be coached?

Will coaching help you reach your professional goals?

What does the coaching process look like? Feel like?

What outcomes can you expect from regular coaching?

Can you coach yourself? Is that really a thing?

How do you find the right coach for you?

Have you internalized limiting beliefs that have blocked your own progress?

Do you truly understand your own values, interests, and goals?

Do you want to be held accountable...really?

Are you ready to grow?

Arguably, these are the types of existential questions that so many busy, highly successful professionals grapple with, consciously or subconsciously, as they contemplate their own growth and development. This book will help guide you through that critically important process of self-reflection and analysis.

I remember having heard someone say years ago that Tiger Woods spends millions of dollars each year on "golf lessons." Admittedly, if that's true, they're most likely not the type of "lessons" you or I would get, but the statement still initially landed for me as somewhat counterintuitive. But the more I thought about it, the more it made complete sense. When you have a continuous improvement mindset, as all world-class athletes certainly do, coaching becomes more important, not less. I'd argue that the same holds true for the best of the best in any field. What separates them is that they view excellence not as a destination but as a journey—a perpetual one—and they're always in pursuit.

— Dana Brownlee, President, Professionalism Matters, Inc.

# Introduction

I think there is a lot of magic and miracle work in coaching. And the art and science of coaching are much misunderstood and often underestimated.

It is not just the way the coaching process works but the very idea of a coach. We may look as though all we have to do is sit and listen and ask a question now and then. In fact, we are admonished by our training not to do too much of the work. "Leave the work to the client," our trainers tell us. The truth is that there is plenty of work for the coach. But what does the coach actually *do*?

We keep time—and not just minute by minute so that we can abruptly interrupt your flow with a brash "Our time is up." We let you know where we are and check in on progress. As much as we can, we bring the session to a "soft landing," leaving you with things to think about, maybe act upon, but not leaving you hanging.

We listen for themes—insights and topics that come up again and again.

We observe and highlight shifts in energy—excitement, lethargy, enthusiasm, and dismay.

We maintain a safe space for whatever you want to express, which is sometimes a rollercoaster of emotions.

We keep your secrets, always honoring the confidentiality and trust of the relationship.

We remind you of your goals and help you adjust them any time you change your mind.

We focus exclusively on you until it is time to stop.

We stay connected with your story between sessions and connect the dots throughout the arc of the coaching relationship.

We tailor our approach to take account of the uniqueness of you.

We temper personal curiosity ("Tell me about your job") while using curiosity to expand your awareness ("What do you need me to know about your job for me to be helpful?").

We look at things from your perspective while inviting you to look at things from a different point of view.

And, believe me, it takes more energy to withhold an obvious piece of advice than to share it. But we know that as tempted as you are to ask for the solution, your success will feel sweeter when you come up with your own plan.

We challenge, encourage, and cheer for you, and we celebrate your wins.

And then we reset and do it again for the next client.

I wish I could more effectively communicate the value of coaching and the investment we make to be good coaches. I make the case for coaching to coaches all the time. I have been privileged to train more than 60 coaches in my career!

But I was surprised to be invited to write this book, because this book isn't for coaches. The intention of this book is to pull back the curtain on the coaching process and to give you, the potential coaching client, an insight into what coaching is about and why you might want some for yourself.

When I first started to write this introduction, I was going to describe you, the audience, as the "potential coaching beneficiary." Apart from that sounding academic (pompous), I realized it is also not a fair representation. As a coach, I learn a tremendous amount *from* my coaching clients. Through my clients, I have learned about changing my mindset, changing my habits, identifying what is meaningful in life, making healthy choices, learning to let go—and the list goes on. It is not because I did not know the theory behind these things and more; it is because there is a big gap between the "what I want/need to be and do" and the "how I am going to get myself to do it and be it."

My wonderful coaching clients have shown me not just where the path is but how to walk it while wearing the wrong shoes and having left my compass at home. As a result of my interactions with my clients, I have changed my eating, drinking, exercise, and sleeping habits. I have narrowed my work focus, identified what matters most to me, and put my energy into those parts of my life. I have made tough choices and built greater resilience and stamina. I have seen how my clients have struggled and succeeded—or adapted—and this has inspired and informed my own journey. For the sake of yourself *and* your future coach, I hope you will embark on the coaching journey. Both of you will benefit!

I hope my clients receive as much from working with me as I receive from working with them. Some of them helped me put language into the journey that is coaching. It is a brave thing to do because it exposes their vulnerability, but it is what this book needs to reach its audience. So, thank you!

## Navigating the Book

This book is split into three sections. The first section, Chapters 1–3, focuses on how to identify your meaning and purpose, why you should want to, what it means to be in your own way, and how to get out of it. If your sense of meaning and purpose is clear, you might find this section less relevant. Maybe you have already explored the questions in this section. No problem. Just jump to the second section, which includes concrete suggestions.

The second section, Chapters 4–8, explores the challenges of creating a life of meaning and examines how coaching can help you get out of your own way. The suggestions in this section are more concrete, and you will see a lot of opportunities to measure the progress of your journey.

Then, Chapter 9 brings it all together (coaching, meaning, and action) and explores how you can create the life you want—how *you* can transform.

In the Conclusion, we will consider the next steps. You will also find some tools in the appendices that will help you decide who you want to be in coaching, how you want to show up, what you want to focus on, which behaviors you want to cultivate and which you want to dial back. We will cover what tools you need to build awareness and to discover new learnings and new ways of being, and how to find *your* coach.

There are five appendices as follows:

Appendix A – Proposed core competencies for coaching clients

Appendix B – Profile of Tegan – one of our case study clients

Appendix C – Profile of Jamal – the second of our case study clients

Appendix D – Suggested questions for selecting your coach

Appendix E – Identifying what is, and is not, a coaching moment

Throughout this journey, I will be working with Tegan (she/her) and Jamal (he/him). Through their experiences, we will examine what coaching is, how it works, and what the results are. To find out more about Tegan and Jamal, check out their profiles in Appendix B and Appendix C, respectively.

Each chapter concentrates on a theme for coaching. Whether you are a potential coaching client seeking to understand what a coaching process might look like for you or a coach wanting to better explain coaching to a potential client, each of the chapters elaborates on one idea—Hope, Strength, and so on. Each of the chapters provides resources for coach and client alike. The book taken all together is a possible pathway to growth and learning through coaching.

### Chapter 1—Finding Meaning & Purpose: Inspiration

When we inspire, we draw people into our journey—or theirs. We connect them to their path, which is what this book is meant to do. Chapter 1 is intended to inspire you to find your *why* and use the tools in the book, and possibly a coach, to help you grab that *why* and make it your North Star.

### Chapter 2—In Your Own Way: Normalization

One of the most common symptoms that shows up in the coaching "room" is imposter syndrome. Most of us suffer from it—that feeling that at any moment someone will notice that we are not who they thought we were, that we don't know what they thought we knew, or that we cannot do what they thought we could do. And many of us feel like we are the only person in the world going through it. Obviously, everyone *else* is feeling good, right? Chapter 2 discusses the difference between normal, commonplace, and habitual actions/thoughts. I'll explore ways you might be creating obstacles that keep you from being who you want to be and what you can do to stop.

### Chapter 3—Getting Out of Your Own Way: Improvisation

Although Chapter 3 explores some Holy Grails of coaching (things coaches hold dear), there really are very few rules. Thank goodness coaching is a forgiving art and science. Coaches improvise and use their intuition, experience, and training. Every client is different, and every day is different. Sometimes that improvisation proves fruitful and provides the client with an aha moment, whereas other times the client shakes their head or looks perplexed. But if we have a good coach-client relationship, good standards, and good intentions, that's okay.

I improvise a lot in this book. Some things will land well and others will make you perplexed. Either way, feel free to write to me if you want to follow up.

### Chapter 4—Appreciating the Coaching Journey: Co-Creation

To get the most out of coaching, the client and the coach need to be ready to co-create the journey together. The coaching client gets to determine what is important, what goes into the agenda, and where the attention is focused. And the coach, if the relationship is going to be fruitful, keeps that agenda in mind, builds the framework, and walks alongside the client as together they draw the client's roadmap.

In this book, we will journey together. I will offer questions and examples, and I hope that you will come to appreciate, in all senses of the word, the journey.

### Chapter 5—Being Hopeful: Expectation

To make progress, we need hope. Chapter 5 explores what hope is—and isn't. We will examine some common misconceptions about hope and shatter some illusions about it. More than wishing, we will make it so!

### Chapter 6—Being Strong: Motivation

Many clients come with blind spots. They don't really know what makes them special. They don't know what drives them. And they don't always recognize that their special qualities *are* special. Chapter 6 measures different types of strengths and explores how you can be motivated to *act* on those strengths.

I am motivated to act by you and by the hope that you will make discoveries as you read this book—about yourself, about what is available to you, and about what meaningful contribution you are motivated to make.

### Chapter 7—Being Brave: Conversation

One of the coaches who advised me in the writing of this book said, "Remember to explain that the best coaching is compassionate *and* tough." And it is true: You will not make changes, discover new things, or make difficult decisions if your coach keeps you squarely in your comfort zone. The ways of thinking you have used before will result in the same outcomes. So, clients have to display a certain amount of bravery in the coaching conversations. Bravery shows up as an openness and willingness to change perspective, but it does not mean a lack of fear or a feeling of comfort. Bravery is feeling uncomfortable and doing it anyway. Chapter 7 explores why bravery—by both the client *and* the coach—matters in a successful coaching relationship.

### Chapter 8—Being Curious: Exploration

At the heart of great discovery is exploration. If we only see the same things we have seen before, think the same things we have thought before, feel the same things we have felt before, and do the same things we have done before, then we will get the results we got before. By being curious about what else is possible, we open up possibilities. One of a coach's best tools is targeted curiosity—not curiosity for the coach's sake but on behalf of the client.

Curiosity happens to be one of my strengths—sometimes to my detriment—so I hope you will see throughout this exploration a healthy curiosity about you, about coaching, and about how to find meaning.

### Chapter 9—Creating Your Meaningful Life: Transformation

Once you know what you want and what is standing in your way, and once you have explored and discussed your options with your coach, found inspiration, improvised, identified your motivation, and recognized how you act in similar ways to other people and how you are different, then it is time to create your new pathway. As you do so, you transform from who you were to who you want to be.

### Conclusion—Choosing Your Next Act: Intention

To finish, we will bring all the pieces together and work on setting an intention. In true project management fashion, we will set an immediate intention, a habit-forming intention, a habit-building intention, an intermediate intention, a moderate-term intention, and a long-term intention. You determine the time frames, milestones, measures of success, and inflection points (when intentions will be reviewed and adjusted). Your journey starts now!

Let's begin!

# Starting with Who You Are

## In This Part

# Finding Meaning & Purpose: *Inspiration*

I have learned over the years that when one's mind is made up, this diminishes fear; knowing what must be done does away with fear.

*—Rosa Parks, Civil Rights Activist*

## The Meaning of Meaning

One of my book advisors admonished me for the way I originally wrote this first chapter. "Don't assume that we are all searching for meaning," she said. "I and others like me already have a strong sense of meaning, purpose, and belonging. We are not all lost in the wilderness!"

There is much evidence that a sense of meaning is a precondition for a long, fulfilling, and happy life. Some of us already have a strong sense of meaning and belonging. We know that people who belong to communities, churches, spiritual groups, and other groups with shared interests and beliefs report living better and longer.[1,2]

So maybe you already have that deep sense of meaning. For the rest of us, it may well be an ongoing search. I know it has been for me, although every day I feel a little closer to clarifying what it is in life that gives me meaning.

How often do you check in on your sense of meaning? One way to measure it is to use an assessment such as the Meaning in Life Questionnaire (MLQ).[3]

Another option is to use a spectrum like this one below and see where you feel you live on that spectrum. If you have a strong sense of meaning, you may want to skip this chapter and go straight to Section 2. Have more questions than answers about meaning? This chapter is for you!

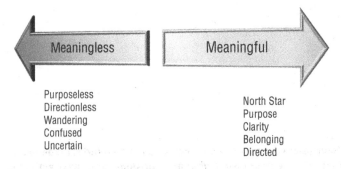

Meaningless

Meaningful

Purposeless
Directionless
Wandering
Confused
Uncertain

North Star
Purpose
Clarity
Belonging
Directed

## Case Study: Tegan

Tegan (she/her) is a middle manager in an information technology company about 5–8 years away from retirement. Before becoming a manager, Tegan was an individual contributor, widely regarded as the go-to person in one of the organization's primary product lines.

Tegan has been offered coaching through work. She has received multiple reassurances that this is not a reflection on her performance. The company is experimenting to see what benefits derive from offering coaching.

---

[1] See, for example, WebMD. (n.d.). Spirituality may help people live longer. www .webmd.com/balance/features/spirituality-may-help-people-live-longer

[2] See, for example, Alimujiang, A., Wiensch, A., Boss, J., et al. Association Between Life Purpose and Mortality Among US Adults Older Than 50 Years. *JAMA Netw Open*. 2019;2(5):e194270. doi:10.1001/jamanetworkopen.2019.4270

[3] https://fetzer.org/sites/default/files/images/stories/pdf/ selfmeasures/PURPOSE_MEANING-MeaninginLife.pdf

It has been difficult to hire and retain people, and someone in HR suggested that an organization-wide coaching program could be beneficial to increase retention.

Tegan has explained that each step in her career has been the result of a manager tapping her on the shoulder and saying, "You should do this next." Tegan's family has big dreams that one day Tegan will run a department, maybe even a company. Tegan enjoyed being the subject matter expert previously but since becoming a manager has felt rather jaded and disconnected from work and the people she works with. That feeling of lack of direction has spread into other parts of Tegan's life, so this coaching presents an opportunity to take stock and reevaluate her choices. Tegan has even been wondering if it is time to change companies.

Tegan has had one meeting with her new coach and established that the coach feels like a good fit. Tegan has been reading about people who feel engaged at work and something called *job crafting*, and she is curious to explore further.[4]

Together, Tegan and the coach come up with an overarching agenda for coaching: "finding my why/looking for inspiration." The coach asks why that is important, and Tegan reflects for a moment and says, "Because I will give more and get more out of life if it feels meaningful, and that will make it easier to navigate tough times."[5]

After a few more moments of thought, Tegan adds, "I don't want just to *look* for inspiration and meaning; I want to find them!"

The coach asks what successful coaching will look like. Tegan thinks for a moment and says, "I will have a plan for what is next that will create a life that feels satisfying and worthwhile. I will be motivated to get up in the morning and feel that what I do each day—or at least some part of it—is worthwhile. And instead of dreaming about retirement and looking for ways to accelerate it, I will relish the days I have left at work."

The coach makes a note not just of what Tegan says but the energy with which Tegan expresses it (and a reminder to explore options for early retirement if the topic comes up again).

## Finding Inspiration

*Inspiration* is a great word. We often talk about it in coaching in terms of what drives us to make a change or to keep doing what we are committed to—what gives what we do and who we are meaning.

---

[4] For an overview of what job crafting is, see Jane E. Dutton and Amy Wrzesniewski, What job crafting looks like. Harvard Business Review. 2020. `https://hbr.org/2020/03/what-job-crafting-looks-like`
[5] Tegan's profile is available in Appendix B.

**6**   Section 1 ▪ Starting with Who You Are
Simon Sinek, an author and motivational speaker, says, "Very few people or companies can clearly articulate *why* they do *what* they do. By *why*, I mean your purpose, cause, or belief. *Why* does your company exist? *Why* do you get out of bed every morning? And *why* should anyone care?"[6]

I also like the other meaning: to draw in. We usually use it to mean drawing in a breath, but in coaching I like to think of it more broadly. It is the process of being drawn into the journey, the inquiry, the exploration, and the implementation of what is possible.

Sinek goes on to say, "People don't buy *what* you do; they buy *why* you do it. We are drawn to leaders and organizations that are good at communicating what they believe. Their ability to make us feel like we belong—to make us feel special, safe, and not alone—is part of what gives them the ability to inspire us."[7]

What draws you in?

If there is one thing I have learned in my years of coaching and, before that, managing people, is that just about all of us want to believe that there is some reason to do the things we do, learn the things we learn, struggle, and stretch. We want to feel inspired to act; we want to be drawn in, not pushed, compelled, or obligated. Tegan is not alone in that.

As a manager, I found that my team accomplished more, felt better, and were more motivated when we were connected to each other and to the purpose of the project. They felt their work was valuable. They sought meaning, and meaning came through connection, purpose, and a feeling that it matters. They were drawn into a common endeavor and felt that they each had a part to play.

In coaching, clients show up at the door for many reasons, but at the heart of most of their visits is the question, "What is my point?" We can rephrase this as, "What draws me in?"

The actual questions they arrive with are varied. Their questions might be soul-searching:

Who do I want beside me in my life?

What next?

What is life balance for me?

How do I feel fulfilled?

---

[6] Sinek, S. (n.d.). *How great leaders inspire action.* TED Talk. www.ted.com/talks/simon_sinek_how_great_leaders_inspire_action/c
[7] Ibid

How can I make better choices?

How do I make others listen?

What is my story?

How do I build confidence?

What is my legacy?

Am I cut out for this?

Or their questions might be practical:

Where should I work?

Should I downsize my house?

How do I get fit? Lose weight?

How do I make a new habit stick?

How do I . . .?

What are your biggest life questions?

## What Is Meaning?

I asked my book advisors to help define meaning. And it turned out to be quite difficult to pin down. Here are some of the answers:

> *"Meaning is behind the things that give us purpose. And when we align to our purpose, we find motivation and satisfaction."*
>
> *—Julianne Wolfe*

> *"[Meaning is]. . . a question of both gut instinct and machination. For me, 'meaning' is having depth and force. It need not be long-term, because this isn't a helpful measure, and life can be transient—and that's okay. I know something is 'meaningful' to me if it resonates and sits comfortably. It is not about 'right' and 'wrong' in any objective sense. I think 'meaning' is, therefore, on balance, a very personal thing."*
>
> *—Sarah Schütte, Solicitor-Advocate*

*"Meaning to me is about the purpose and your desire to achieve it. Meaning explains why you want to meet and exceed goals."*

*—Diane M.*

*"Meaning answers the question, 'Why am I here?' I would add that meaning helps us to find a way to feel that there is purpose in our life, work, relationships."*

*—Jana Wardian, making meaning by being Nana and researching to reduce the work of being a patient*

## So, What Is Meaning?

Michael Steger is one of the foremost researchers in the field of "meaning."[8]

He has described meaning in life as follows:

$$coherence + purpose + significance$$

Coherence is our understanding—what we think about who we are and what we do. It is the way that we create connections between one experience and another, between one person and another.

Purpose is why we do it, where we are going, our ultimate goal(s).

Significance is a sense that our beliefs, goals, and actions matter.[9]

When we understand where we are going and why, and when we are clear about what we are pursuing and feel that it is important and valuable, we have meaning. We are inspired!

## Why Does Having a Sense of Meaning Matter?

There are probably many people in the world, often people with reasonable resources, who cannot identify what gives them meaning. They do the things they do because those things are the next steps on a path

---

[8] For example: Martela, F. & Steger, M. (2016). The three meanings of meaning in life: Distinguishing coherence, purpose, and significance. *The Journal of Positive Psychology*. 11. 1–15. 10.1080/17439760.2015.1137623

[9] Frank Martela & Michael F. Steger (2016) The three meanings of meaning in life: Distinguishing coherence, purpose, and significance. *The Journal of Positive Psychology*. 11:5, 531–545, DOI: 10.1080/17439760.2015.1137623

defined by someone else; they bend to the opinions of others; and they barely pause to reflect on what matters to them. And there are people with few resources who have a great sense of meaning. Then there are those of us who are lucky enough to have both resources *and* a sense of meaning. Which do you want to be?

When we have a sense of meaning, the next steps seem inevitable. Despite fears, we are drawn forward. Despite setbacks, we keep going. With a sense of meaning, we tend to become more hopeful, more adaptable, more curious, and braver. We can go beyond the boundaries of what we previously thought we were capable of.

There are many descriptors for meaning: our North Star, our guiding light. Whatever you name it, the concept is the same: It is the reference point we always come back to. Regardless of how far we wander, the fundamental meaning of our life brings us back on track. Unless we don't have a sense of meaning.

What then? Does life end? Not always, but it can become a bit of a drag. We can feel as though we are wandering aimlessly, not really knowing how or what to choose. Or maybe we accept someone else's idea of what is meaningful. We may seek short-term thrills to up the excitement. In the end, however, without our own sense of a North Star, most of us feel pointless, unfulfilled, and empty.

## Meaning Is Personal and Not Always Constant

Over time, our sense of meaning may change and evolve. Some things that drove me as a child no longer provide motivation. I would do my homework so I could go out and ride my bike. Now I do my homework so that I can connect more people to their purpose. I can draw more people into their lives. Other childhood drives, such as learning and applying new things, still provide the same sense of forward motion and satisfaction.

I am not talking about a biological imperative here—to reproduce, to survive. I am talking about a sense of something that we can focus on, feel, and return to. It is understanding what makes it worth being here, feeling that being here is contributing something, and that what we are contributing matters. It is the sense that we matter and what we choose to do matters too. Maybe it is even the sense of "If I don't do it, who will?"

Meaning is personal and cannot be imposed by someone else. However much a parent or teacher may want us to want to be a brain surgeon, they cannot *make* it so, regardless of how much they may try. And they cannot make us passionate about the idea.

Indeed, many of the people I coach are working to identify the gap between who they are, who they want to be, and who others want them to be. All too often they have felt pressured to follow a path laid out by someone else. They come to coaching looking for ways to identify and be driven by their own personal sense of meaning.

Some clients are seeking a complete sense of meaning.

Others know what makes sense to them but question whether it is significant enough. Or they are driven to go after something but cannot explain why. Or they do things that seem to give value to others but cannot see what the end goal is.

When they have all three components of meaning (coherence + purpose + significance), they know who to be, what to do, and where to go next, even if it is difficult.

What makes sense to you?

## What Are Some Ways to Find *My* Meaning?

Discovering your own sense of meaning generally requires reflecting on a lot of questions. We will use some of them in this book, and maybe along the way you will have some aha moments, some insights—or maybe you will decide you want a coach! If you need help discovering your life purpose, don't worry. While some of us already have a strong sense of meaning, most of us struggle to put a finger on what it is that matters most to us.

When I changed my career a few years ago, I *found* more meaning. Rather than deciding what gives me meaning and going after it, I ran away from a role that was taking away all sense of meaning. Initially, I had found meaning in being a project manager, as project managers are part of the reason that projects come to fruition, and that felt mean-ingful. But we don't always get to work on the life-changing projects. Many are mundane. They may be important to someone, but they may not have broad importance.

Project managers contribute in many ways, but in my last project as a program manager, I discovered my passion: people. It was not clear to me at first. I just observed the times when my energy was high—and when it was not—and I noticed a correlation between people and energy. Anytime I interacted with others, listening closely, asking questions, or challenging assumptions, and saw what seemed to be a lightbulb moment, a smile in the darkness, a "Wow, I would never have thought of that," an understanding, an insight, or just a sense of relief, my energy lifted.

It surprised me because I am innately an introvert. It surprised me because I did not feel I had any special skill in "people." But others disagreed, and I already knew that people fascinate me. Why on earth do we do what we do? Why do we choose what we choose, even when we don't think it is the choice we want? And interacting with others in ways that causes shift, change, or a reconsideration is, quite frankly, thrilling.

I became my own experiment.

Now it is time for you to experiment. How do we start to coach for meaning? What might that mean in a coaching session?

Here are some questions I might ask in a coaching session where the client says they want to discover their meaning:

What does *meaning* mean to you?

When do you have the greatest sense of meaning?

How will life be different if you have a greater sense of meaning?

On a scale of 1–10, how much sense does your life make to you?

What would it take for that score to be one point higher?

What does it mean to you for life to "make sense"?

In what ways does your life make sense to you?

On a scale of 1–10, how motivated are you to get into your day?

What would it take for that score to be one point higher?

What makes you get up in the morning?

What is there in your life that feels like you are making a valuable contribution?

On a scale of 1–10, how strongly do you feel that you have a life worth living?

What would it take to make that score one point higher?

Consider the following exercise. Take a piece of paper and write for 5–10 minutes without worrying about spelling, punctuation, or language. Just write. You are not going to share this with anyone. It is more effective if you write by hand, but if that is not comfortable, you can use a computer. But *write*!

I feel the greatest sense of understanding, purpose, and significance when I

_____

_____

_____

_____

_____

Put the writing away for a couple of days and then reread what you wrote.

What did you discover that you did not already know?

# Who Are You in This Life?

What energizes you?

Are you mindful about who you are each day?

Do you make mindful choices or just go through the motions on auto-pilot?

How do you take stock of who you are versus who you want or expect to be? How do you measure your progress? What is your current goal?

I am not talking about comparing yourself to others—the conversations we have with ourselves about what old friends or enemies are doing now, how "successful" they have been compared to us, and whether we seem to be on track with our onetime peers. I am talking about knowing what *you* mean to be.

A few years ago, one of the people I am privileged to call part of my audience messaged me and asked, "How do I become like you?"

I was startled. No one had ever asked me that before. In fact, despite the many privileges I enjoy, I have often thought that it is good no one else has to be like me! Then, frankly, I became a little dismissive; after all, we cannot be someone else. It is just one of those hypotheticals that does not really get us anywhere. Then I got curious about the question. Who am I? Why do I bother? And then beyond that, what draws me in? What is meaningful to me?

I spend almost every day helping others find out who *they* are, and yet I realized in that moment that I did not really have a clear vision of who I am or who I want to be.

I have always been fascinated by what motivates us. And yet here I was, not really knowing what motivates me. I decided to explore.

## Starting at the Beginning

One of the first exercises I did was at a racism awareness training. The task was to write down who I am, measured by roles such as race, gender, home role, nationality, native language, professional role, education, income, family roles, and other personal roles. Then I had to reflect on the journey I had taken: the people who had influenced me for good and bad, people who had challenged me, and some who had misinformed me, experiences of travel, nature, exhilaration, and despair. I am the sum of all that and more.

There are many potential categories to explore, but in writing this chapter I set a goal of filling a page or so with attributes. It took about 5 minutes. The result follows.

What do you notice? One thing that stands out to me as I look at the list is that I have not identified a profession or job. Curious. Most coaching clients gravitate quickly to what they do for a living as an identifier. What is on your list?

| CATEGORY | ROLE/LABEL |
|---|---|
| Race | White |
| Appearance | Blue eyes, red hair (natural), moderate build, 5'6" |
| Gender | Female |
| Sexual preference | Open |
| Children | 0 biological (by choice); 2 adopted/step |
| Primary family roles | Wife, stepmother, grandmother |
| Secondary family roles | Sister, daughter, sister-in-law, daughter-in-law, absent aunt; in early life, cousin, niece, granddaughter |
| Other roles | Friend, colleague |
| Primary language | English |
| Mindset | Curious, challenging, skeptical |
| Mental health | Lifelong anxiety, occasional depression |
| Education | Postgraduate |
| Influencer: mother | White; first-generation college; grew up during World War II, experienced rationing and evacuation; three older siblings; no intention to have children; childcare officer, probation officer, social worker, family therapist |
| Influencer: father | White; first-generation college; grew up during World War II; one older sibling, who died before my father was born

No intention to have children; traveler, speaker, industrial scientist |

*Continues*

*(continued)*

| CATEGORY | ROLE/LABEL |
|---|---|
| Influencer: paternal grandparents | Irish; many siblings; lived in poverty; grandfather war veteran (WWI) |
| Influencer: maternal grandmother | Maternal grandfather died in 1944; grandmother married, widowed, never remarried; four children; ran a boarding house; one of three siblings |
| Influencer: sister | Married, three children; family-oriented, driven, and with full career in education in the UK |
| Location of upbringing | UK—rural Kent, London, New York |
| Education | All-girls school in Gravesend, Kent; engineering university in Bath (to study economics!), England; London School of Economics to further study economics |
| Educational studies | Economics, law, mediation, coaching, positive psychology, project management, finance |
| Role models | Early life, mainly male: my father, a science teacher, a boss, a professor; later life, increasingly female: actresses, authors, teachers, artists, activists, friends, colleagues, women who overcome, women who shine, my mother, my daughter, my sister |
| Anti-role models | Bullies, dictators, politicians, women who undermine other women, bosses, teachers |
| Passions | Nature, reading, learning, movies, believing in others, music, challenging assumptions, stirring the pot |
| Health | Generally good; used to be very physically active (mini-triathlons, squash, circuit training); now lazy about exercise; love healthy food; strong history of dementia on mother's side causes concern; father's family physically healthy, has some mental health challenges |
| Socioeconomic status | Middle class |
| Living situation | Own home, shared with one person |
| Living conditions | First world; running water, city sewer; high level of general comfort, many conveniences, access to healthy food, clean air, outside spaces |

## What Does All That Mean?

I am not a religious person, although I do consider myself to be spiritual. I feel strong connections to nature, people, trees, and more. I also have a strong sense that our choices can have big ripple effects. But I don't believe we are meant to follow a preordained path. Our choices are often limited, but we do get to choose—if not what to be, then *how* to be.

As I contemplated the who am I question, I realized that the more urgent question for me is, what am I supposed to do with all that life? How do I combine the various parts of my life to construct a meaningful path forward? What lessons am I going to learn, and how will I apply those learnings? What feels significant, important, purposeful? At the end of my life, what do I want my legacy to be?

In positive psychology one of the exercises we use is to have people imagine that it is the end of their life (a little morbid, I know) and they are writing their epitaph. What would you like it to be?

What words do you want on your epitaph?

*Here lies Ruth. Throughout her life she looked for the better side of people's nature, their strengths, their skills, and helped them to see and activate their better nature too. She brought out the best in people. She was not perfect—far from it—but she always maintained a sense of meaning and believed life is worth living.*

What do you want *your* legacy to be? What do you want said about you? What words do you want people to use about you?

---

**Perhaps one never seems so much at one's ease as when one has to play a part.**

—*Oscar Wilde*

---

What part do you want to play? You cannot play me, and, honestly, you would probably not want to. But you can become whoever you are meant or want to be. Sometimes it is hard to do. Alone, it is hard enough. How can you develop perspective, challenge your own thinking effectively, consider options you don't know exist? As Socrates famously said, "The more I know, the more I know nothing." The expanse of what we don't know will always be greater than that which we do know.

So, we turn to others to help us, right? Of course. But the problem with others is (a) they are usually trying to find themselves and their place in the world and (b) if they care about us, they care about what we choose to do and be because they have a vested interest and generally want to influence us.

Our parents want us to go to college, get a good job, "be happy." Our life partners want us to want the things they want, to share in the journey, and to care for them. Our boss wants us to want to stay in our job and perform well.

Or maybe we just don't like to ask for help from anyone, and we struggle on alone.

A frequent challenge is that we make choices when we know the least and the people around us think they know more. We choose our school focus before we know what we want to do and be. We choose a life partner before we know who we are. We choose where we live based on where we have already been. We may get where we are meant to be going in the end, but it is a less than efficient journey.

# Case Study: Tegan

What about Tegan and her search for inspiration and meaning?

One of the striking aspects of coaching is that we go where the client wants to go. Tegan has already identified areas of exploration: values, character strengths, skills, and motivation. Although many people assume that the coaching relationship is one where the coach leads and the client follows, the opposite is true. The coach uses the breadcrumbs left by the client to help them uncover the path forward.

## A BRIEF DISCUSSION OF ASSESSMENTS IN COACHING

Many coaches feel compelled to use assessments to help move the conversation along. And there are some great ones out there, which I will mention as I go along. My caveats though are fourfold:

1. Assessments and their debriefs are not coaching; they are a form of information gathering. Ask your coach questions about the purpose of the assessment and only spend time on assessments that align with the type of information you want to gather in the course of your coaching.

2. In my opinion, assessments should only be used as the relationship develops. Beware of any coach who leaps to an assessment before you have even started the coaching engagement, unless you have signaled that a particular topic—emotional intelligence, for example—is a key focus and agree that measuring your current level is helpful. Assessments are often useful, but they need to

be selected by coach and client together and in the context of what is most useful to *you*.

3. In my opinion, assessments should only be considered when you have expressed an interest in knowing more or have asked if there is a useful tool for measurement. The opportunity to use an assessment should be driven by you and your coaching curiosity.

4. Very few things can be achieved with an assessment that cannot also be achieved with pure coaching. The primary one is to get a measure of where you are now so that you can measure progress.

## Values

Values might be described as guiding principles; they are the ideas we hold about how life is and should be. They are the principles that are hard to compromise—when we are fully aware of and committed to them.

So how do we discover a client's values? Of course, one way is to use some sort of assessment.

While this can be useful, storytelling with observation can be even more powerful.

Tegan's coach decides to use the storytelling approach and considers a few prompts to get the conversation going:

How much have you already thought about your values, and what have you discovered?

When did you feel the best about yourself during the last week or two?

What did you make sure you did and make sure you didn't do?

Tell me about a time when you felt you were being true to who you are and what is important to you.

What part do you want to play?

Of course, many follow-up questions are possible, depending on where the client goes with this exploration. The main role of the coach is to listen carefully and observe—because this is a chance to hear in the client's story what matters to them most.

The coach goes with the last question: What part do you want to play?

Tegan thinks for a few minutes while her coach sits in silence. Then Tegan responds, "When I was in school, I advocated for changes to some of the school rules that seemed out of date and prejudicial. It was scary to speak up and make waves, but it felt good. I want to be an advocate in the workplace. I am not quite sure what this means yet, but I want to make the working experience of my team members positive and safe."

## Character Strengths, Motivation, and Engagement

Business leaders and human resources became more focused on the idea of motivation and engagement when Gallup started publishing their statistics on workplace engagement. We quickly came to realize that most people did not feel connected to their work or inspired to give more than the minimum. Indeed, a significant proportion of the people surveyed were actively disengaged, which can mean that they are spreading negativity. Gallup showed that there is a correlation between how much we use our character strengths and how engaged we feel at work. And managers have a special role in cultivating that engagement.[10,11]

Over the time I have been coaching, one of the most powerful skills I have learned is to help clients identify their strengths. All too often coaching clients are focused on what they lack, what does not work, and they cannot see the strengths—the positive parts of their personality—with which they are endowed.

A colleague of mine, Dr. Robert Biswas-Diener, describes strengths with a sailboat metaphor. Weaknesses are imperfections in the hull, maybe even leaks. We want to patch the weaknesses to make sure they don't sink the boat, but they don't make the boat go faster or more directly to where it is meant to go. Strengths are what fill the sails and drive the boat to its destination.

This is not just an opportunity to give positive feedback to the client or just a way to boost their ego. It is an evidence-based approach that helps us to explore both the best—and possibly the not so great—about the client.

Again, although some great assessment options are available, so much more can be discovered through coaching conversations.[12]

---

[10] Beck, R. & Harter, J. Managers account for 70% of variance in employee engagement. Gallup.com. Retrieved April 30, 2023, from https://news.gallup.com/businessjournal/182792/managers-account-variance-employee-engagement.aspx

[11] Gallup, I. State of the global workplace report. Gallup.com. Retrieved April 30, 2023, from www.gallup.com/workplace/349484/state-of-the-global-workplace-2022-report.aspx

[12] For example, the VIA Character Strengths assessment from the VIA Institute on Character (Free); Strengths profile from Cappfinity; and the much-used corporate tool, Clifton Strengths from Deloitte. Each measures something slightly different and provides different insights. The VIA is particularly helpful in teams and groups, because the basic assessment is free and there are some great ways to look at the profile of the team as a whole.

Tegan's coach considers options:

Tell me about what it is like to play the part you described for yourself?

How does it feel?
Who are you with?
Where are you?

What are you using to bring forth the best in yourself?

Tell me about a time when you were at your best.

In the next chapter we will explore what it means to be in our own way.

---

**REFLECTION QUESTIONS FOR *YOU* TO PONDER**

- What part do you want to play? (What is your *why*?)
- What parts do you *not* want to play? (What is your *why not*?)
- What have you done, been, or said in your life that most inspires you?
- What are you inspired to be?
- What will you learn from those previous inspirations?
- What's next?

# In Your Own
# Way: *Normalization*

---

**If you are always trying to be normal, you will never know how amazing you can be.**

*—Maya Angelou*

**When you find people who not only tolerate your quirks but celebrate them with glad cries of "Me too!" be sure to cherish them. Because those weirdos are your tribe.**

*—A.J. Downey*

---

When I started this book and chose the title for this chapter, I was thinking exclusively about how we get in our own way. We are most likely to be the biggest obstacle to our own progress and success. Long-held and often inadvertently reinforced beliefs cause us to limit our own horizons. Outside expectations and commitments to other people prevent us from considering new perspectives. And often, we don't know where to find the resources we need to support change.

Once I started to write, I realized there are two sides to "in your own way," and both are at the heart of coaching.

Of course, what most often brings someone to coaching is that they have something they want to accomplish, and they need support in creating and executing a plan to take them from where they are to where they are going. Accomplishment looks different for each person. For one it might be getting a promotion; for another it might be having someone to act as a thought partner to help them develop ideas and question beliefs; for another it might be implementing a health plan; for yet another it might be authoring the book they have long dreamed of writing.

Whatever they are seeking, something is stopping them from making the journey unaided.

Maybe they have tried before and have not achieved the outcomes they wanted, or maybe someone else—such as a manager or HR—is recommending coaching to "solve" a perceived problem. Either way, we are coaching you to get out of your own way and become the person you want and have the potential to be, whether that is an elite athlete, a C-suite executive, an effective communicator, a more confident dad, or someone more hopeful and braver.

The other side of coaching is our focus on *your* way. As I mentioned in the Introduction, coaches often have ideas about how their clients should move forward. We have seen other clients with similar goals taking similar roads. But they are never identical, and we learn in our training and through experience that unless you travel your journey in your own way, you won't get where you want to go. We can offer you examples of maps that other people have used, but my journey or the journey of another coaching client is going to look very different from yours.

One of my coaching teachers uses the example of meeting a friend over coffee. They are having a challenge in life and meet to ask "advice" from you as their friend. You give it your best shot, the benefit of your wisdom, and tell them what you would do—or have done—in the past. There are four possibilities:

1. They do what you suggest—in my experience, the least likely outcome—and it works! Yay! But now they feel dependent on you. They come to you more and more when life's challenges arise.

2. They do what you suggest (or at least they do what they thought you were suggesting), and it doesn't work. They are frustrated and wonder why they ever asked you in the first place. Maybe this impacts your friendship over time.

3. They may or may not seem to listen and then do something else entirely—and it works. Your advice seems wasted, and you wonder why you bothered to put your energy and effort into their problem in the first place. You have enough problems of your own!

4. They do something else entirely, and it does not work.

We are much more committed to our own beliefs. Often, we don't really want someone to give us a new suggestion; rather, we are hoping they will affirm what we are already thinking of doing. This is known as *confirmation bias*, where we filter what we see and hear and give greater emphasis to the things that align with what we already believe, want, or feel.

One of the biggest surprises for new coaches—especially those who have previously been trainers or teachers—is that it is their knowledge of and dexterity with the coaching process that is most important to the client, not their knowledge and experience of the client's world. As coaches, we know that often the *last* thing we want to be for coaching a client is an expert in their field. It makes it hard for the coach not to offer specific suggestions and hard for the client not to request them.

In coaching, instead of advising, we are focused on questioning:

1. What are your values?

2. Which choice is true to who you are?

3. What will your future look like if you make one choice or the other?

4. We use scales to help you measure the strength of your commitment and emotion—for example, on a scale of 1–10, how confident are you?

5. We ask what is in the way and how you can overcome those things.

In the end, *you* choose the path; we help you spotlight your best choices. Having chosen your goal and your path, we help you create a plan to embark on the journey.

## Being in Your Own Way

One of my favorite movie scenes is in the George Clooney movie *Up in the Air*. As he is discussing with someone (the incomparable J.K. Simmons) that they no longer have a job, he asks, "How much did they first pay you to give up on your dreams?"

Yes, it is a movie. Yes, it is a romantic notion. Yes, many of us realistically face big obstacles—maybe insurmountable ones. Some of us have unrealistic dreams. We need the support of others; we need lucky breaks; we need to work hard. But I still think it is a valid question—and one that coaches ask, in one form or another, all the time. And we also provide the reality check to help you identify which dreams are to be pursued and which are to be, well, dreamed!

It takes a lifetime of training and experiences to develop our idea of what is "normal." Some things we are told by parents, other relatives, teachers, friends, and even newscasters, magazines, and TV shows. Other things, we observe, often assuming that what happens to us habitually is "normal." How would we know otherwise when we have nothing to compare it with? Children growing up in unusual circumstances assume their situation is normal. And children that grow up in run-of-the-mill circumstances also think their experience is normal. And what we think is normal tends to be what we think everyone else is experiencing.

We tend to believe that what happens *to* us is normal. And yet, as a coach, I observe that we tend to believe that what happens inside us— the things we think and feel about ourselves and our experiences—is anything but normal.

"I am too shy. Other people walk into meetings with such confidence."

"I am so emotional. I wear my heart on my sleeve. Other people are much more together than I am."

"I couldn't do that! I am nowhere near as capable/smart/knowledgeable/ clever as other people."

"I always screw up because that is what I am, a screwup."

"Eventually someone will realize that I should not be in this position— that I am an imposter."

Even if we believe what we are experiencing is "normal" and everyone goes through it, at the same time we often believe we are far from normal in who and how we are being. Other people have it nailed and we are somehow odd, broken, or dysfunctional.

Coaching, then, is a delicate balance between helping you to identify the things you have in common with others and helping you identify the things that set you apart!

## Case Study: Tegan & Jamal

Tegan and Jamal are attending a group coaching session. There are eight people in the group, and the topic is hope (which is explored further in

Chapter 5, "Being Hopeful: Expectation"). Everyone in the group breaks into pairs to explore what hope means to them. For some, it is wishing; for others, it is seeing tomorrow as better than today; and for others, it is faith. One person even says it is having the belief that when we go to bed, we will wake up the next day!

As the group comes back together, Tegan's partner in the breakout exercise reports (with Tegan's permission) that Tegan had shared a personal story. She told a story of a time when she and her family were at the dinner table and her father asked, knowing that she had studied hard and was a good student, "So, did you get a good grade on your test?"

"I hope so," replied Tegan, tucking into some mashed potatoes.

"Oh, no!" replied her father. "We don't do hope here! You either do what you need to do—or you don't!"

Jamal is astonished and raises his hand. The coach asks what he would like to share.

Jamal replies, "My household was like that! I have never heard anyone describe that before. I almost did not come to this group session because the topic was hope, and I was raised to believe that hope is empty, frivolous, and pointless. My friends at school used to make fun of me and call me Minor Misery because I would tell them that hoping was a waste of time. It is good to know that I am not the only one! I am curious to know what we are going to discover about hope today."

Tegan smiles and says, "Yeah, I suspect we are going to find there are other ways to think about hope!"

When clients discover they are not alone, it is very often the first step in changing their mindset. Hearing someone else describe their experience can help us see the reality of it. For example, when Jamal heard Tegan's story, it helped him start to question whether hope is as worthless as he had long believed. (The research suggests it is not!) Hearing it from someone else, far from confirming it, gave him an opportunity to reconsider it and decide that that point of view is too narrow and unhelpful. It helped him to become more curious about other ways to look at and think about hope. Both Jamal and Tegan started to question whether what they had been brought up believing might not be 100 percent true!

## Normal vs. Average

Much of the information we use to drive decision-making is based on averages. Education is often designed for the average student; medical treatments are designed for the average patient. For example, my husband

and I received the same dose of the COVID-19 vaccine. I am lighter than he is, so it was no surprise that he had no reaction and I was knocked off my feet for a day! Everyday items are designed for people of average height and weight. We work on the premise that the average IQ is 100 and then generally assume that our own IQ is higher than that (which necessarily means that at least one person's IQ must be lower than 100).

Sometimes this works as a decent benchmark or starting point. Often, we must supplement with "special" programs to bridge gaps. But just as often, if not more so, average suits no one. The counter is too high for some and too low for others. The medication is too strong for one person and does not put a dent in the pain for another.

In coaching, we are not looking for the average or a middle ground suits everyone (and no one) perspective. Instead, we seek your unique path, which involves identifying the following:

- Opportunities to help you see that you are not alone in your experiences, beliefs, desires, and habits—to *normalize* your position. It is hard for anyone to make changes if they believe they are an anomaly.

- Ways to challenge your normal so that you can consider new directions and approaches. We can look at where the beliefs come from and research other possible outlooks.

- Pathways designed for *you* to make the progress or changes you desire. A coaching pathway, though it may look similar among clients, is not an average; it is unique to you. We develop it together, adjust it along the way, and tailor it to who you are.

## Normal vs. Universal

A client came to me and said, "It has been two years since my partner died, and I still feel as though it was yesterday. I cannot focus; I don't want to go out; I feel adrift—even though I know she would want me to be getting on with life, I just don't feel ready. Occasionally I have moments when I feel enjoyment or even a little optimism, but it always seems to come crashing down later when I realize that she is gone forever."

Another client came and said, "It has been two years since my father died. We were very close, but strangely I feel whole. I feel as though he would want me to be getting on with life. I feel his presence and remember the things he used to say to me. There are times when I feel sad that he is gone, but overall, I feel ready for my next chapter, even though it is without him."

Representations of journeys—whether they be journeys of grief, change, learning, recovery, or growth—tend to show us a steady path forward, with predictable progress and a predictable sequence. As many of us already know, these representations are convenient but generally inaccurate. The truth is that no two journeys look identical. They may look similar at points in time, but dig into the detail, and they are at least as different as they are the same.

As coaches, we are not looking for a universal experience. We recognize and celebrate the uniqueness of our clients. We help them to see that even if they are not like everyone, they are likely to be similar in some regard to several "someones."

## Doing in Your Own Way

This personalized coaching pathway is what I mean by the second perspective on "in your own way." It is doing things in the way that suits you. Although coaches are sensitive to who you already are and what you are comfortable with, they also challenge you to change.

Doing things your way does not mean always doing things the same way. You can learn from past experiences—and this may or may not be doing things the way you have done them before. We look for things that work and reevaluate things that don't.

In coaching, you adapt your way and from time to time create a new way for yourself, replacing unhelpful beliefs and habits with new, helpful ones. You become incrementally more effective at living your life.

It is your journey to travel as you wish, and the coach is here to help you travel it well!

## Psychological Flexibility

As I was writing this chapter, I came across a social media post by one of my favorite mentors, Dr. Todd Kashdan, that examined psychological flexibility:

> [Psychological flexibility]...refers to a number of dynamic processes that unfold over time, including how a person: (1) adapts to fluctuating situational demands, (2) reconfigures mental resources, (3) shifts perspective, and (4) balances competing desires, needs, and life domains.[1]

---

[1] Kashdan, T. (2023, September 8). *Todd Kashdan on* LinkedIn: www.linkedin.com/feed/update/urn:li:activity:7105882602087043072

It reminded me of an aha moment I enjoyed a few years ago when I discovered that Charles Darwin had identified adaptability as the precursor to survival—not fitness, at least not in the sense I had always assumed. We are not born or made to be "fit" for our experiences. We learn, grow, reconfigure, and rebalance.

While we may be wedded to "our way," psychological flexibility enables us to adapt our behaviors and change the story we tell ourselves. Adaptability, doing things differently over time, becomes our new "normal."

On our own, however, it can be hard to recognize unhelpful thinking. Believing that what we are doing now may not be the best choice does not mean we recognize the alternatives. Our "normal" often gets in the way.

Coaching is a resource that supports adaptation, reconfigures mental resources, offers new perspectives, and helps us to navigate the balancing act so that we can effectively prioritize our wants, needs, and life domains. For example, how many coaching clients want to find "work-life balance"?

# Case Study: Tegan

When Tegan first considered coaching as a resource, she was not sure what to expect. Some people she spoke to said the coach would tell her what to do in order to accomplish her goals. Others said that coaching is "wishy-washy" and feels nice but does not achieve much.

But when the opportunity to try coaching came up at work, Tegan, always one to use available resources, decided to try it out.

Tegan explains to her new coach that she has been quite satisfied with life for the last few years but that recently she began feeling that there must be more to life. At the same time, she reports often feeling tired and lethargic, which is getting in the way of her exploring her options.

Tegan wants to feel more satisfied with life but also believes she must continue to earn a good living and support her family.

The coach invites her to explore what has changed since she felt satisfied. Tegan lists the following:

1. We have been in Brazil for an extended period. When we first came, it was so new and interesting. I still love the people and the country, but the novelty has diminished.

2. Our daughter left for school in the United States, so it is just the two of us.

3. My boss asked me what my plans are for retirement. I don't think he was trying to pressure me or get me to quit, but sometimes

when my male bosses approach me about work, I get defensive. It took a long time to reach my level. I don't want to feel that I have to rush out of the workforce.

4. My partner retired and took up painting. She has been taking a lot of classes and has been traveling all over. This year, it was to the south of France; next year, she is going to Italy.

The coach waits. Tegan reflects.

At last, Tegan says, "Well, I suppose that is quite a lot of change! I had not really paid attention. I just process one thing at a time and don't always notice the cumulative effect. I just get on with what is in front of me."

Tegan's coach asks her how being specific about the changes helps her to reevaluate and change her perspective.

Tegan thinks some more and answers, "Well, I can see that I need to be kinder to myself. My tiredness is understandable. I am getting used to a lot of changes, and sometimes that just takes all the energy I have. But I think it is time to reevaluate what these changes mean for me. Each of them presents opportunities!"

Tegan is starting to think about the resources she has and how to consider new perspectives. She is already showing psychological flexibility.

## An Aside on the Opportunities of Groups

In our earlier case study, Tegan and Jamal were attending a group coaching session. Unlike the experience of a focused one-on-one session, where it is just you, your story, your goals, and your coach, group coaching has some advantages—and disadvantages—for some. But when it comes to being in your own way, especially due to normalization, groups can be a great alternative—or addition.

Tegan and Jamal were asked what was most appealing to them about the group coaching option. Here are some of the answers they provided:

1. There is safety in numbers. If I don't feel like saying much, I can sit back, and someone in the room might have an idea I can try.

2. Hearing the perspectives of others is helpful. Often, what I hear from other attendees gives me new ideas—not only about what I might do but also things I don't want to do. They have tried it, and from their feedback, I can decide not to invest time in doing the same thing.

3.  When I hear someone play back what they have heard me say and compare it with an experience they have had, that is often enough for me to reconsider my perspective. It distances me from my thinking and beliefs and helps me be objective.

4.  Attending group coaching over an extended period, we naturally started to network, and I felt that my circle of connections and supporters grew.

5.  The coach is great, but she generally does not offer solutions to the challenges I am facing. She has explained that as the coach, she will introduce strategies that have worked for others, but she will not tell me the steps to solve my problem or achieve my goal, because each of us is on our own journey. The same rules don't apply to the participants. That said, it can be helpful when someone in the group has a similar experience. First and foremost, it helps me feel less like an odd person out, *and* they can often help me prioritize what to do next. Sometimes I think I see a look of relief on the coach's face, as if to say, "Thank goodness *someone* suggested that!"

Other benefits can be accessibility—group coaching can include more people and is usually less expensive than one-on-one coaching. You may also have access to a team of coaches rather than just one individual, providing you with an opportunity to work out what you want from your own coach.

Group coaching is usually developed around a theme that interests all group members. So, you might not always get to explore some of your more personal concerns and topics, or you might not feel as comfortable doing so in front of a group. While group members are generally required to agree to confidentiality, it is much harder to ensure that nothing gets shared, because group members are not usually subject to the code of ethics of a professional organization such as the International Coaching Federation (ICF).

Group coaching is another example of coaching's balance between discovering the ways in which we are similar to others and identifying the ways in which we differ.

Having discussed the two ways in which we are "in our own way," in the next chapter we will explore how to combine the best of the way we do things with ways to get out of our own way.

## COACHING QUESTIONS TO MOVE YOU FORWARD

Here are some questions to help you consider how you are in your own way:

■ What are some of my core beliefs about myself?

■ When I am talking to myself about my work, efforts, or relationships, what do I say to myself?

■ Who believes in me the most?

■ Who helps me?

■ Who reinforces my own self-doubts?

■ What resources do I need?

■ What will a coach be likely to notice getting in the way of my success?

■ What is something I chose not to attempt but now think I could have accomplished if I had tried?

Here are some questions to help you discover what your own way *is*:

■ On a scale of 1–10, how has your approach to life worked for you so far?

■ How do you like to get things done?

■ Who do you rely on?

■ How do you learn new things?

■ When someone shares a new idea with you, how do you evaluate its validity?

■ How long does it take you to get from a new idea to a new action?

■ If there were one thing you could change about the way you approach life, what would it be?

■ If you were working with a coach, what is one thing they should know about you?

# Getting Out of Your Own Way: *Improvisation*

> Tho tost of a first-rate intelligence Is the ability to hold two
> opposing ideas in mind at the same time and still retain the ability
> to function. One should, for example, be able to see that things are
> hopeless yet be determined to make them otherwise.
>
> *—F. Scott Fitzgerald*

The first time I attended an improvisation class I laughed so much I thought I would stop breathing, partly because the other people were so funny and partly because of just how ridiculously hopeless I was with the most basic prompt: "Yes, and. . ."

"She flew here on her broomstick. . ."

"Yes, and. . ." Long pause. "She asked for a cup of tea."

"Are we in space?"

"Yes, and I am floating in a most peculiar way!" (My mind often goes to song lyrics.)

Even as I struggled to get into the flow, I believed this class would be one of the most impactful I ever attended. Yes, I have been to graduate school, law school, coaching training, mediation training, and more, but this skill of improvisation hit me as the foundation for growth and development—taking "what is" as a starting point and then building from there.

It was also a natural building block to put on top of the topic I discussed in Chapter 2: normalization.

Coaching clients often come to a session struggling with a challenge to which they bring their long-held beliefs. They tell the coach what they should—and shouldn't—be doing or feeling. They castigate themselves for not being stronger, for not being further along in their own journey.

They describe a thought, a feeling, or a belief that disappoints them, thwarts them, paralyzes them.

"Yes, and. . ." the coach replies.

## Reason and Emotion

When people come to a coaching session or workshop, they generally believe they are bringing their "thinking" brain. They hope to learn something new—and they perceive that as an experience in reason. I beg to challenge that expectation.

Learning and growth are most often a whole-person experience. Sometimes when I learn something new, I feel butterflies of excitement in my stomach, my breathing changes, and I wear a smile on my face. My brain is running overtime as I attach my new learning to all the other things filed in my brain. When I am learning, I am mentally and physically "captivated." When a coaching client has an aha moment, they describe feeling excited, elated, relieved, hopeful, focused, energized, smarter, and more capable.

Having observed this inevitable connection between emotion, reason, and learning, before starting any group session, one of my favorite practices is to ask the audience to consider Plutchik's Wheel of Emotions.[1] It introduces a pause, a space, and some reflection, and it encourages everyone to think about something they rarely think about—how they are feeling in this moment. And not just experience it but put a name to the emotions—what psychologists call *labeling*. Most of the time we "feel" how we are feeling. We experience it—and sometimes we feel we can barely tolerate those emotions. It often seems as though we will feel a particular way forever.

---

[1] *File:plutchik-wheel.svg*. Wikimedia Commons. (n.d.). https://commons .wikimedia.org/wiki/File:Plutchik-wheel.svg

Whenever someone is joining a workshop, a keynote, or a coaching session, they are coming from somewhere else. They have been interacting with others or spending time alone. They have been happy, frustrated, sad, feeling accomplished, and more. Whatever they were feeling travels—at least to some extent—into their next encounter, their next meeting, their next idea.

Plutchik's Wheel of Emotions—the daisy shaped diagram below—is a simple tool. Although it does not claim to identify every possible emotion, it provides a great framework for exploration.

The audience receives the following instructions:

1. Spend one minute reviewing the wheel.
2. Which emotions are you feeling in this moment?
3. Make a note of them—no need to share.
4. Look out for experiencing multiple emotions.
5. Look out for conflicting emotions—often about the same thing.

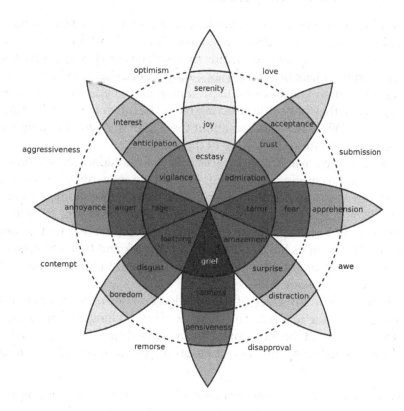

Often at this point I will share that I am both excited and afraid to present, that I am happy to be with them and anxious about how this is going to go.

We then sit in silence for 30–60 seconds and reflect.

Finally, I invite everyone to think about what they noticed and to choose which of their emotions they want to check at the door and which to bring with them into the rest of the session. Having completed the exercise, we jump into the session. Maybe we are learning about and exploring hope, character strengths, or coaching skills. Whatever the topic, we are *not* analyzing, challenging, or trying to change how we were feeling at the start. We just get on with the session—together.

We have shared an experience and yet experienced it individually—privately. We have linked reason and feeling. We have primed ourselves to be who we want to be in this moment for this session. We are ready to learn.

## Accepting Conflicting Truths

When I first introduced the emotions exercise in my sessions, many people were startled to discover another layer of emotions under the obvious ones. Many people assume they will have experiences that are all or nothing, black or white. When they realize that they admire the speakers for their knowledge and presentations, they are nervous about the playback they have promised to give at the lunch next week; it is an eye opener. While they are sad about the loss of a loved one, they also smile at the memories they have of them.

In her 2014 article in *Psychology Today*, Dr. Amelia Aldao[2] shares some of the research on emotions. She points out that we are generally becoming less able to name our emotions—a condition that at its extreme is known as *alexithymia*. She also uses the example of a coworker able to identify their anger at a colleague, but who may overlook the fear that is there too. How many of us have had a bad day at work and then screamed at the kids, or had an argument with a loved one and then burst into tears the first time someone speaks to us?

At one point in my career, I was speaking a few weeks after I had to put a favorite dog to sleep. The thought of her no longer being around and the memory of the moment when she passed still caught my breath, making it hard to speak. Those emotions sat side by side with the

---

[2] Amelia Aldao. (n.d.). "Why Labeling Emotions Matters." *Psychology Today*. (August 4, 2014): www.psychologytoday.com/us/blog/sweet-emotion/201408/why-labeling-emotions-matters

recollection of some of her goofy antics—raiding the trash and bringing me a used tea bag, stealing the topping off a pizza and managing to close the box, burrowing in the snow until her face was caked before running through the dog door and sliding into the kitchen counter. Yes, I was devastatingly sad—so much so that before going up on stage to speak I resorted to burying my head in a pillow and screaming to alleviate the anguish. Yet, I was so happy to have had those years with her. She was hilarious, feisty, goofy, independent, and a huge motorcycle fanatic!

As I write this chapter, it is the 23rd anniversary of my father's sudden death. Yes, I am still sad that he is not here to see what I am doing, cheer me on, and question my wisdom, *and* I am happy he gave me all the things he did that got me where I am now and where I am going. Yes, and. . .

What are the emoticons for happy and sad? Excited and afraid? Love and disgust? Maybe they look something like these:

## Case Study: Tegan

Tegan arrives at her coaching session in a hurry. As she sits down, she says, "I have good news! I have been offered a role in Canada. It will be a promotion. I should be excited—and I am—but I am terrified."

The coach waits in silence.

Tegan continues, "I am excited because it means we get to move again. It feels like it is time for a change. And we will be closer to our daughter, which is nice. It is a long trip for her to visit us in Brazil. I had been thinking I might have to get ready for retirement, so when they started exploring this role with me, I was very surprised. I will be managing a team that will be creating a startup under the umbrella of our parent company. It is a service providing mental health services to high schoolers and college students. Apparently, they have been researching the needs and opportunities for some time and feel it is a good time to get into the field.

"I have never had an opportunity to work on something from scratch and certainly did not expect such an opportunity to come up now! And with a daughter in college and my own experiences with therapy, coaching, and medication, this feels like it aligns so well with what is important to me. And I think it will set me up for the next stage of my life when I am retired and can volunteer my time."

Tegan looks up toward the ceiling and smiles to herself, "Maybe I will become a speaker on the topic of mental health. Maybe I will write a book or record a TED Talk!" she says excitedly.

She continues, "In my most excited moments, I see myself with my team accepting an award for something to do with the new organization. I picture myself surrounded by young, energetic team members who appreciate my lived experience and longevity but also love that I am open-minded and willing to experiment. And we are joined by people who can share testimony as to the effectiveness of our service. And I will learn something new and be able to offer something valuable to other people!"

Tegan stops speaking and looks expectantly at the coach, who says, "Yes, I feel your excitement. And. . . ?"

"And nothing," answers Tegan hastily, taking a pause before continuing.

"Well, I do have some doubts. This does not feel like my area of expertise, and some of the team members have already been seconded from other roles. There will be a lot of networking and relationship building with other organizations in the field. I do enjoy networking, but at the same time it is daunting. What if this endeavor fails? When I am not picturing awards and smiling faces, I see us living in a tiny studio apartment eating instant noodles out of plastic containers. What on earth makes the leadership think I'm a good fit for this job?

"It is weird, and I am excited and terrified at the same time. I want to go to Canada and get started as soon as I can, and yet I keep thinking about handing in my notice and taking early retirement. I wish I could feel one thing or the other, then I would know what to do.

"Am I right to want to take this role or am I making a horrible mistake? Sometimes I think if this were the right move, I would have no reservations. I would *know*, wouldn't I?"

The coach draws a breath and asks, "On a scale of 1–10, 1 being not at all, 10 being very, how excited are you about this opportunity?"

Almost before the question is finished, Tegan answers, "An 11!"

The coach continues, "And on a scale of 1–10, 1 being not at all and 10 being very, how scared are you by this opportunity?"

"Hmmm, I suppose about a four. No, probably a three."

In the silence that follows, Tegan begins to smile. "I think I can handle that!" She laughs.

## What If Every Choice Is Right—and Wrong?

Clients often tell me they want to know the "right" thing to do. "How will I know if I was right or wrong?" they ask. Offered a choice between two or more options, they are sure that one of them is "right" and the others are "wrong" and that the challenge is to identify the "right" one.

"Am I doing the right thing?"

"Am I making the right choice?"

"Was I right to challenge my boss like that?" or "Was I right to keep quiet?"

"Was I right to ground my child for two weeks?" or "Was I too lax when I only took away their phone for a day?"

Experience with those same clients has shown me that there is rarely one right way when it comes to choices. And even what generally turns out to be a good choice has its downsides and entails some sacrifices, because every decision involves saying yes to some things and no to others. Rather than searching for the "right" way, we have more success when we can recognize that all we can do is make the best decision possible, at the time we need to make it, based on as much information as we are reasonably able to acquire. At a different time, we might make a different choice. With different information, we might go another way.

Tegan's fear may provide insight into the gaps in her knowledge, and once she identifies those gaps, she can create a plan to deal with them.

All her feelings are data points to consider.

Telling your boss what you think may alleviate some stress, may make you feel more authentic, and may result in a healthy change at work. Keeping quiet may give you time to consider other options, gather more evidence, or win the trust of someone who is going to be important to you long term.

And, unlike when I was testing systems in the financial services industry, we don't generally get to run two versions of our decision in parallel to see which one works out best. We rarely get test runs!

Coaches encourage clients to explore what can be *learned* from their various thoughts, feelings, and questions. We challenge our clients to measure their priorities—and to measure the intensity of their emotions. Often, this is by using a simple scale from 1–10. Other times, maybe there is an assessment to help. Just as labeling emotions can help us come to grips with them, sizing them up can help us get perspective. What may feel like an overwhelming pressure suddenly seems more manageable when we recognize that on a scale of 1–10 this stressor is a 4, 5 or even a 6 or 7, and we know we have handled higher levels of stress than that before.

At the start of this chapter, I talked about focusing on "what is."

Tegan's coach could ask questions about how she feels, challenge her on what she is afraid of, or ask questions about previous times when she has experienced mixed emotions. Instead, she asks the following question:

"What is true for you now?"

Tegan thinks.

"Well, there is a list:

1. I feel as though I am stuck in a rut.

2. I want a change—a new place and a new role, maybe both.

3. My partner is on board, at least based on what she has said.

4. I don't want to retire—maybe ever but certainly not now.

5. No one has ever actually said I have to retire. That is a story I am telling myself.

6. There is a new opportunity, and it has the potential to be a good one.

7. The new opportunity does build on my skill sets, but it is also a stretch role. And that is exciting!

8. It aligns with who I am and what is important to me.

9. It is not the first time I have been offered something that has scared the c\*\*p out of me. When I look back, I realize that when I moved to Brazil, I thought I had lost my mind!

10. No decision is forever. I could change my mind if it does not work out.

11. I will not be thrown in on my own. There will be a board of internal and external advisors with experience setting up similar programs.

12. I don't think I have ever had a colleague at this organization who I just could not work with. They don't all become my friends, but I don't think I need any more friends right now!

13. Some of my greatest successes have come through the things I have been the most anxious about.

14. Staying in my current role would mean I could coast to retirement.

15. I do enjoy parts of the role, even though a lot of it feels like autopilot.

16. My current role provides a lot of flexibility, and I have the energy and focus to do things outside of work because it does not take all my energy.

17. If I stay where I am, we are probably in pretty good financial shape for the rest of our lives.

18. My partner has mentioned she would like to go back to school and then back to work.

19. I don't look back on any of my choices and think they were "wrong." I sometimes think I could have been more considered and more deliberate, but every choice has led to something good, even if there have been difficulties too.

20. I am generally adaptable!"

As Tegan makes her list, her breathing slows, she looks more comfortable, and she says, "I am sure there will be bumps along the way, but we have always managed. I am in! I won't ignore my worries, but I won't let them get in the way, either."

"Your concerns are information," her coach replies. "What are they telling you?"

## There Is No Magic Recipe for Success

Read a self-help book or a book about mental health, and you will often be presented with the "best thing" to develop; seven steps to accomplish something; the five habits that successful people adopt. Whether it be self-compassion, boundary setting, building a network, reading something daily, taking a month off in the summer, or understanding your character strengths, I find that many of my coaching clients are looking for *the* thing they should focus on to ensure success. Sometimes they tell me about a book they are reading that is providing them with "the answer."

At one time everyone was emphasizing grit. The work by Angela Duck-worth[3] certainly provided evidence that people with grit—a combination of passion and perseverance—accomplished more. But what happens when perseverance becomes wasting time and energy or when passion becomes unhealthy obsession?

Other writers and researchers espouse positivity, hope, love, and more. We have at times even had a formula for the right balance of good and bad feedback, positive and negative experiences. We also know from cumulative research that we tend to gravitate back to a particular level of well-being that is somewhat habitual for us. (Notice that I didn't say "natural" or "normal.") This process—known as *hedonic adaptation*—and the point we get to—often referred to as the *well-being set point*—are generally attributed to a combination of genetics (50 percent)[4] and cir-cumstances (10 percent)[5], and the leftover is attributed to the choices we make and the behaviors we adopt (40 percent)[6].

Don't get me wrong: I love reading about these ideas. I am always curious. But I am also skeptical—because I am pretty sure there is no one right thing and certainly no magic recipe. Each idea offers another piece of the puzzle. Each idea has its time and place. And each idea brings with it the risk of too much of a good thing.

Too much self-compassion can become self-indulgence or selfish-ness. Too much curiosity may become "shiny new thing syndrome"—something I am prone to myself—an inability to focus and get anything done. Boundary setting may become selfishness and not leave enough space for others' needs and wants.

Our interactions with others are always a delicate balance between being enough of ourselves and leaving enough room for others.

Today you may need more self-compassion, whereas tomorrow you may want to think less about yourself and your immediate well-being and instead be focused on others. This week may be about stimulating curiosity, whereas next week you might need to dial back curiosity and

---

[3] Angela Duckworth, *Grit: The Power of Passion and Perseverance*. (New York: Scribner, 2016).

[4] Julia Braungart et. al. "Genetic Influence on Tester-rated Infant Temperament as Assessed by Bayley's Infant Behavior Record: Nonadoptive and Adoptive Siblings and Twins," *Developmental Psychology* 28, no. 1 (1992): 40–47.

[5] Michael Argyle, "Causes and Correlates of Happiness," in *Well-being: The Foundations of Hedonic Psychology*, eds. Daniel Kahneman, Edward Diener, and Norbert Schwarz (New York: Russell Sage Foundation, 2003), 353–373.

[6] Sonja Lyubomirsky, Kennon Sheldon, and David Schkade, "Pursuing Happiness: The Architecture of Sustainable Change." *Review of General Psychology* 9, no. 2 (2005): 111–131.

focus your attention on your goals and commitments. Today you need to experience your grief; tomorrow you need a distraction.

One of the benefits of a coach is that we can help you find the balance you are looking for, the right amount of each ingredient for each new situation, experience, or desire. We can even help you test whether the latest idea is "real," whether it really merits your attention and effort, or is just a distraction. We can ask you how you are likely to feel about something in a week, a month, a year and help you realize that something looming large today will probably recede into obscurity in a relatively short amount of time.

I once attended a coaching class that explored strengths—one of my favorite topics. The topic was how our personal strengths may be unlikeable or upsetting to someone else. Honesty without a teaspoon of kindness and a tablespoon of social intelligence may seem like cruelty. Conversely, kindness without honesty may seem like lying. What makes it complicated is that our intent is not enough. We may intend no harm, but the recipient may experience the intensity of our strengths differently. I know, for example, that when I get intensely curious, it can feel to others like the Spanish Inquisition even though I don't mean it to. Clients say I am not for the faint of heart!

We need to be sensitive to the impact of our strengths on those around us. We want to read the signs to minimize the risk of unhelpful friction. But just how far do we go in moderating our own behavior out of respect for others, and how much should we protect who we are and be authentic? We did not come up with a definitive answer, but I am curious to explore more, and that is one of the topics we often do explore in coaching with our clients. How much should we stand our ground, and how much should we give ground, and how does the answer change, based on the circumstances and environment?

Is it the job of the coach to be more reticent in their questions, or is it your job to find a coach who feels more comfortable to work with? It is a bit of both, I suspect. As coaches, we ask permission to share stories, ask especially challenging questions, and to dig deeper; as a client, you choose your coach. Some people work with the same coach on multiple facets of life. Some people keep the same coach for a long time. Others change coaches as their needs change and their preferences develop.

Someone asked me once, "What is the usual length of a coaching engagement that the client said was beneficial?"

I had not considered that question, and rather than trot out the usual answers—typically 3–6 sessions minimum, but it depends on the client, the topic, and the goals; it is whatever it needs to be—I decided to check my coaching records. Just how long are most of my coaching engagements? The answers surprised me.

The shortest coaching engagement was one session of 20 minutes. The client expressed their satisfaction by giving a written and a recorded testimonial. The client had one goal, and as soon as the goal was achieved, we were done. We stay in touch, and for all I know they work with other coaches, but our coaching is done—for now.

The longest engagement has been more than two years and is still ongoing. The focus of the coaching has morphed over that time, and my client says they continue to find working with me beneficial. From time to time we explore the value of a new coach, and the client decides each time that for now they don't want to change anything.

Be open, be curious, and periodically take stock to make sure that coaching is still providing what you want. Sometimes it is time to take a break; sometimes it is time for a new coach; and sometimes it is time for a different professional.

## It Is Not Just the Client That Must Get Out of the Way

This chapter has concentrated on the coaching client. I started Chapter 2, "In Your Own Way: Normalization," by suggesting that coaching clients are often our own worst enemies. Our self-talk can be just as, if not more, damaging than the things that others say. We can talk ourselves out of success—often more easily than we can talk ourselves into trying.

It does not stop with the coaching client, though. The coach can get in the way, and their ability to cultivate psychological flexibility, not just in their client but also in themselves, has a significant impact on the coaching relationship and the outcome.

Great coaching is not a role for the faint of heart. People come to coaching looking for change, validation, innovation, liberation. They want to be heard, challenged, reassured, and to feel understood and appreciated. There are very few small goals in coaching, because most goals entail the client changing their thoughts, habits, and/or beliefs. And the client often trusts the coach with the most personal details, the most intimate and private thoughts and ideas and beliefs they don't share with anyone else. You want to be open to possibilities and curious about what those possibilities are. You need to be willing to consider that change is possible and be ready to recognize and leverage your strengths, even when you may not even know you have them, and be willing to be at least a little bit brave. Coaching is, after all, not always comfortable.

What if your coach is full of self-doubt?

What if they wonder if they can help you?

What if they doubt that they have enough experience, enough insight, and will know the right questions to ask?

All these thoughts and more may get in their way, and indirectly in yours.

Coaches *are* human (at least most of them), so doubt is natural and even, in the right measure, healthy. Who wants an arrogant coach? (If you do, that's fine!) At the same time, there are some things you might want to explore with your coach.

## Recommendation 1

Ask your coach the following questions. (See also Appendix D for additional suggestions.)

1. Who coaches you?
2. What do you do to hone your coaching knowledge and skills?
3. What do you think the role of the coach is?
4. How comfortable are you not knowing the answer or the outcome?
5. What do you do if you get stuck in a session with a client and don't know what to ask or say next?
6. What do you do if you feel like you asked the wrong question or made the wrong comment?
7. What do you do if you are having an off day?
8. How do you feel about clients changing coaches?

I share my answers to these questions later in the chapter, but they are just one set of answers from one coach. Rather than describing how I think coaches should respond, I invite you to consider what you want the answers to be. I do personally believe that a coach who is not coached or does not have access to a mentor is a coach who is unlikely to develop. Some coaches do reciprocal coaching with other coaches—that is, they receive coaching in exchange for providing coaching. Others have a supervisor or a coach they consult. Still others participate in coaching groups where there are demonstrations of coaching and opportunities for being in the hot seat and getting advice. Many of these coaching opportunities are offered by the coaching associations (e.g., ICF) or coaching schools themselves.

I also believe that a good coach wants the best outcome for their client. Sometimes that means moving on and working with a new coach.

## Recommendation 2

Interview other coaches from time to time to see if your needs have changed or another option is available. This gives you a chance to see what you are missing and may be a chance to rediscover how special your coach is.

## Recommendation 3

Own the choice of your coach. Recommendations are great, but what makes a coach special for *you* may be very different from what makes a coach special for your friend, family member, or colleague. Most coaches offer an introductory session—use it. You don't just want to be sure they are the coach for you; you also want them to know that you are the client for them.

## Recommendation 4

Define the attributes you want in a coach, how you will measure success, and the process for ending or changing the relationship. Having the framework in place ahead of time can make it easier when you feel like a change. Agree to regular check-ins when you and your coach can work together to evaluate the ongoing benefits and opportunities.

One of the times that coaches experience mixed emotions is when their client is ready for a pause or to stop. Coaches generally enjoy seeing the growth and development of their clients. Ask your coach how they proceed when the coaching relationship comes to a pause or to the end.

---

**MY RESPONSES TO THE QUESTIONS IN RECOMMENDATION 1**

As I was answering these questions, I realized that many of them could be answered with the word "improvise." Coaching has lots of guidelines and few rules. Whether I am at a loss for what to ask next or feel like I have said something I wish I hadn't, the "yes, and. . ." mindset is my go-to. Yes, I wish I said something different, and I will move on from here.

The following answers are my personal reflections. Ask me on a different day or when I have coached more people, and they might change subtly. I suggest these are some ways to think about the questions I posed. They are not the only answers, and I certainly don't consider them to be the "right" answers. They are hints of the beliefs I coach by.

1.  Who coaches you? *Coaching is such a powerful resource that it would be strange to me to be a coach and extol the virtues of coaching without availing myself of its benefits myself. I admit I am surprised when coaches don't have a coach themselves or don't at least consult with fellow coaches.*

    *I am fortunate to have a big network to draw from. There are people around the world with whom I exchange reciprocal coaching. I know very experienced coaches who will always spend time exploring options and challenging my thinking. They are always ready for an ad hoc meeting to tease apart the threads of a challenge or a decision in front of me. Most of the year I am participating in coach training to enhance my skills. I also have a network of non-coach colleagues who are happy to discuss how they would want a coach to coach them.*

2.  What do you do to hone your coaching knowledge and skills? *I am passionate about coaching, so I spend a lot of time reading, studying, reviewing new research, and attending coaching webinars, demonstrations, and training sessions. I explore other topics to broaden the reach and impact of coaching, such as neuroscience, law, communication, education, and more. As a speaker to other coaches, I learn a tremendous amount both preparing for a session and from participating with other coaches in the session. The adage, "see one, do one, teach one" has a lot of relevance in our profession.*

3.  What do you believe the role of the coach is? *This book is part of the answer to this question. I listen closely and ask questions to help you decide if you are being who and how and you want to be, and if not, what you want to learn and to change to get closer to your ideal. I am a supporter—but not a cheerleader.*

4.  How comfortable are you not knowing the answer or the outcome? *When I started as a coach, I thought I was supposed to "know" what the client needed to do. Now I am comfortable not knowing, and I am curious to see where the client will take us. One of my favorite things is when I ask a question and the client answers it in a totally unexpected way. For example, I once asked a client what he thought was going through his child's mind during a time of conflict. He surprised me by answering in relation to a totally different child. And that opened a completely new avenue of exploration for us both!*

5.  What do you do if you get stuck in a session with a client and don't know what to ask or say next? *One of my favorite tools is silence. There are times when I need a moment to think through what my client has said, or when I am not sure what question would be most helpful next. I will keep quiet while I think about it. Often the client offers a new idea or new thought themselves. And their thoughts and ideas generally get them closer to their goals—or at least help them understand what is standing in the way. Also, I have learned that there is no right question and that the coaching process is quite forgiving. If a topic is*

*not fully resolved or explored, it will likely come up in another coaching session. That presents an opportunity to notice the recurring theme and explore its importance for the client.*

*Occasionally I will ask the client what question would be most helpful to them, or what they would ask if they were in my shoes. If they have just been talking about a long-held belief or an assumption they are making, a question about what would be different if that assumption is wrong may nudge things forward.*

6. What do you do if you feel like you asked the wrong question or made the wrong comment? *As I previously mentioned, I don't subscribe to the idea that there are right or wrong questions. If I ask or say something that seems to cause offense or upset my client, I will acknowledge the change in energy and ask them what is happening in that moment. Sometimes I will say something like, "That was not a very coach-like comment. May I try that again?" Another question I will use is "What do you wish I had asked (or said)?"*

7. What do you do if you are having an off day? *My first concern is that my client have an effective coaching session. Not all sessions are created equal, and either or both of us may be experiencing something that negatively affects the session. That said, I don't want to cancel or reschedule sessions at the last minute. Usually I will ask the client what they would prefer. I let them know as much as I can about the situation and ask them how they would like to handle it. I always remember a day when I was in a very blue mood and did not want to get out of bed. The only thing that got me going was a client session in the afternoon. I forced myself to get up and shower and then met the client, and we had a productive session (based on their feedback). It was not just they that benefited, it completely changed my mood. As a coach, I don't want to compromise the experience or the value for my client, and at the same time, dependability is important.*

8. How do you feel about clients changing coaches? *I think that everyone and everything has a time and a place. I might be the right coach for you now, but later you might want or need someone else. Or maybe I am not the right coach in this moment but at some later date will seem to be just the right one. My primary goal is to ensure that you have the best coaching experience you can have. Sometimes that may mean working with me; other times it may mean me introducing you to other coaching options.*

*One of the most challenging things for me as a coach is to inquire about what the client needs. I want them to be able to consider different coaches and be open if they think it might be time for a change, but I don't want them to feel as though I am suggesting they should change coaches.*

*When a client comes to the end of a coaching engagement, it is a time of mixed feelings for me. I love to see the progress that clients make, to see their growth, and to witness their successes. At the same time, it is a great milestone when a client feels ready to take a break or make a change. Honestly, I often miss my clients—even the ones who I don't work with for very long. But there is a deep satisfaction in knowing that you have been alongside someone on a part of the journey and hopefully made that journey easier in some way!*

# Where We Are Going Next

Section 1 of this book explored the concept of meaning and the ways we can get in—and out of—our own way both as clients and coaches.

Section 2 will consider some specific practices and skills that my clients have found useful. As previously mentioned, I don't believe there is a perfect recipe for success or a specific set of skills we should all focus on; however, the four topics discussed in Section 2—hope, strengths, bravery, and curiosity—are a good foundation to get you moving forward on your journey!

Why these four?

I encourage people to understand hope for two reasons. First, I believe most of us have misconceptions about hope and mistakenly believe it is a passive state, confusing it with wishing or believing in external factors. Second, when we can cultivate hope, we can start to see possibilities for the future, choose them for ourselves, and devise pathways forward. And by considering the pitfalls of hope, we can ensure that we stay grounded and don't leave too much to fate.

Knowing our strengths is a great way to see what we already have in our toolbox. As we learn more about our strengths and how we can cultivate and optimize them, we discover we have more choice and capacity to be who we want to be. Also, by looking at the benefits and pitfalls of strengths, we can ensure that we are dialing them up and down as we need to.

Bravery is often misunderstood. When we underestimate our levels of bravery, we underestimate our capacity for change and growth. If we can tolerate just a little extra discomfort, we can reach up a little further. That said, we want to ensure that we are brave, not reckless, and that we recognize when to step away.

Curiosity is a key tool for discovering new options. Curiosity benefits both the coach and the client, but it needs to be the right type of curiosity. Coaches should be more curious on the client's behalf than to satisfy their own desire for information and knowledge. Clients use curiosity to explore their options.

Section 2 discusses these topics in more detail, including the upsides and downsides of each.

---

**QUESTIONS TO GET YOU OUT OF YOUR OWN WAY**

- What is true for you now?
- If your superhero/heroine were here, what would they suggest you do?
- What is the last thing you did to make progress toward your goal?
- Which things are in your control and which things depend on other people, the situation, or luck?
- What will be different once you accomplish your goal? And what will stay the same?
- On a scale of 1–10, how enthusiastic are you about your goal?
- How did you determine whether the goal is realistic?
- How much will you have to stretch your skills, tolerance of discomfort, and beliefs in order to reach the goal?
- When have you previously stretched your skills, tolerance of discomfort, and beliefs?
- Who do you want in your corner to support you?
- What are your 30-, 60-, and 90-day targets to move you toward the goal?
- Which strengths do you have that make your goal more achievable?
- What is one thing you can do today to make your desired outcome more likely?
- What would you do if you were 5 percent braver?
- What is something you are curious about?

---

# Launching the Journey to Your Future

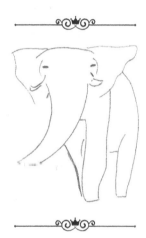

## In This Part

# Appreciating the Coaching Journey: *Co-Creation*

> Coaches are necessary because they help you see a different version of yourself. Coaches challenge you in a way someone who works with you every day wouldn't.
>
> *—SF, coaching client, 2022–2023*

If you picked up this book, you likely are already at least curious about the possibilities of coaching and are open to the idea that, if not necessary, coaches can at least be useful.

People who have experienced coaching are highly likely to say that coaching is necessary or at least that it is beneficial. When I asked past clients to rate the necessity of coaching on a scale of 1 to 5, with 5 being necessary, the average score was 5 (although one person did give an 8).

We can probably all agree that coaches aren't "necessary," not in a general way. Not everyone has a coach, and not everyone struggles because they don't have a coach. And, of course, there is always the possibility that we will work with a coach who is less than effective—at least for us. Indeed, coach-client rapport is the biggest predictor of the success of the coaching relationship.[1]

## Case Study

When Tegan was offered the chance to experience coaching, she was a little hesitant. Stories abound of coaching being used to address behavior and fit issues in the workplace, and Tegan was suspicious. The other coaching stereotype, that coaching is for fast-track people on their way to the corner office, never crossed Tegan's mind. This was partly because Tegan had been in her career for a long time but also because Tegan was aware that her attitude was probably not optimal for her current role. It was unlikely that Tegan's prior career path would continue with someone tapping her on the shoulder once more for the next opportunity. Let's face it, for some time, Tegan had had one eye on the door.

So at first, Tegan was skeptical about having a coach. But after some reflection and discussing it with her life partner, Tegan decided there was nothing to lose.

"Might as well give it a try," Tegan thought.

## Is a Coach Even Necessary? (Or Can I Coach Myself?)

One of my favorite coaching questions is, "Who have you been since we last met?"

One of my favorite answers is, "I have been a better version of myself." After all, this is what coaching is all about, finding out who the better version of you is and then taking steps to be that person.

Even if the answer is a disappointed "I have been a lesser version of myself," it opens up the exploration because then we can look at what small change can be made right now. We may look at what got in the way, and we can certainly look for evidence that the client accomplished more than they may have noticed. And it is a whole lot more challenging than "How have you been since last time?"

---

[1] Carolin Graßmann and Carsten C. Schermuly. *Journal of Personnel Psychology* 2016 15:4, 152–163.

Would you like to find out how to create a string of best moments for yourself? Not that any moment would necessarily be perfect, but in each moment you would choose the path that ensures you would do, be, and feel the best you can in the circumstances. You would be your better self—unless you *choose* to be your worse self. Your choice.

Do you know how to create those moments? Or do you stumble into them from time to time and say, "I wish I could feel this way more often?"

If you can put your hand on your heart and say, "Yes, I can consistently create these moments, and I do," then chances are, you can manage fine without a coach.

For the rest of us, some help is needed. We need someone with whom to talk things through. We need someone to reality check our assumptions and beliefs, and often we need someone to help us keep on our chosen path, especially when the terrain gets bumpy.

Ask what a 1:1 coach is for, and most people will suggest one of two reasons to have a coach:

1.  You are on the way to the top, on the fast track, and your company provides a coach to help develop your potential as quickly as possible. The organization recognizes that you can go further faster with a partner explorer than you will go with just a sponsor, mentor, or manager. That is not to say there is not tremendous value in those people, but they do not provide the same value as a coach.

2.  You are a problem at work. There is a "challenge" (euphemism for "you are getting on others' nerves, upsetting them, or even bullying them). First is a performance improvement plan including coaching; next step, out the door. The organization recognizes that you must be given a chance to change, and that change is most likely to happen with a guide who is attuned to you and supports you.

But for day-to-day living, with all its decisions, priorities, and demands, we *should* be able to get along on our own or with a little help from our friends, right?

I am an adult and know what to do, even if sometimes I don't do it!

This is what I believed when I was starting out on my career and my adult life. Being an adult means being self-sufficient. To ask for help is a weakness. Real grown-ups can manage on their own.

Why is it that some organizations—even ones that come under criticism for so many things—can recognize what we don't recognize for ourselves: that a coach can help bring out the best in us? Even some of the most successful people in the world recognize that they are better with help, support, and someone they can trust to challenge them and bring in a different perspective. If organizations will pay for coaching, there must be a substantial return on investment; otherwise, they would not do it. Why wait for a problem or someone else to give us the opportunity?

I had never thought of a coach as an essential resource until 2012.

That year, in the middle of an intense and important program at a large for-profit organization, I burned out. I went from being a human dynamo to a dead stop. And no amount of self-reflection, self-castigation, or lessons learned from prior experiences got me unstuck. I started to wonder if I needed the help of someone else. I knew I did not want therapy. I had a pretty good idea of the journey that had brought me to this point—and my preconception based on experience was that therapy was about analyzing the past.

---

**On your own, you do your best thinking based on your knowledge of yourself.**

**With a coach, you get to see a 360-degree tour, which enables you to think about a situation from myriad angles; you scrutinize your values and measure your choices against them—and through that you gain self-awareness, options, and purpose.**

*—Irene Poku, Authentic Leadership Coach*

---

I wanted someone who could first help me look forward and then *step* forward. I wanted someone to listen to me, challenge me, and then help to keep me honest. And I needed someone to see what I could not see: my assumptions, my limiting beliefs, *and* my possibilities. More than anything, I wanted someone to talk to who was interested in my story and my progress, my dreams, and choices but was not affected by them. I found that person in a coach, someone who cared and yet didn't; someone who wanted me to make the best choices but was not affected personally by those choices; and someone whose vision of who I could be was not limited by who I had previously been.

Alone, we can get stuck inside our experiences and cannot see them objectively. We may be able to feel them and experience them, but that does not mean we can evaluate them for what they are: a subset of all the experiences possible. Our experiences can seem as though they are *all* that is possible.

So, I would answer, a coach is not necessary, but working with a coach is an advantage. Just in case you have lingering doubts, this chapter explores the role and value of coaches.[2]

# The Role of the Coach

## COACHING HOLY GRAIL #1

**The primary role of the coach is to help the client find agency.**

Part of that is selecting the *right* coach for them in this moment. But clients don't want to work with *any* coach; they want a coach who helps them feel hopeful, strong enough, brave, curious, and empowered. They want a coach who works for them as they are in this moment. What works may change over time, but every time the client seeks a coach, our first job is to ensure that they get the choice of coach they want. We don't know best; they do. To that end, we need to encourage clients to ask questions, and we need to be open to the termination of the coaching relationship at any time. Locking a client into a relationship is not only undesirable but also, in this author's opinion, unforgivable.

## COACHING CLICHÉ #1

**The coach meets the client where they are.**

Clients may have heard that this is a commitment that coaches make, but they are not sure what it means. When you look for a coach, you come with certain beliefs, assumptions, cultural norms, influences, and experiences. It is the job of the coach to greet you as a complete, functioning person. It is not for us to judge you, criticize you, or dispute your beliefs. We are partners with whom you can explore how your current decisions serve you and identify where you want to make changes. And then we can help you stay on track to make those changes. We highlight your progress and celebrate with you, even if we don't personally want the same things. We join you on your journey until you drop us off at a turn.

And if we cannot meet you where you are, or if we start believing that you should be somewhere else, then we must step away.

---

[2] Throughout this book I will be referring to the International Coaching Federation (ICF), the core competencies and the code of ethics as well as the ICF Core Values. The ICF is by no means the only monitoring body for coaches. However, it is (i) A reasonable standard to use; (ii) It is the standard with which I am most familiar; and (iii) It is the standard that the coaching schools at which I have taught and been taught have used.

One of the most common questions asked of coaches is, "How does coaching work?" or "What is coaching?"

Depending on where in the world you are from, you may think of a coach in sports terms—someone with a playbook to follow who teaches you those plays, creates drills to hone your moves and skills, and builds team vision.

Or you may think of a coach as someone who works with you on professional performance or presence. Or maybe you think of someone who works with you to develop your voice, teaching you techniques to lift it up.

This often leads to new coaching clients believing that the coach will tell them the answer, solve their problem, or instruct them on what to do.

However, an effective coach is not an advisor. An effective coach is not a mentor.

Whereas mentors use their personal experience to offer insights into how to navigate specific situations, especially at school, coaches mine your experience, beliefs, and assumptions for what can move you forward or hold you back. After a coaching session, one of your choices might be to consult a mentor for context-specific input into your specific situation. Advisors usually have expertise that they have learned through education, training, and experience, and they believe that they have a solution roadmap (and generally we believe that too). While good advisors or consultants will tailor their advice based on context, they are generally already committed to a way of doing things. That way may feel awkward, alien, or inapplicable to you.

So, what is the point of having a coach, if they are not going to solve your problems and give you the recipe for your success?

---

**Coaches are necessary because we are often unable to hear our inside voice until we use our outside voice with a trusted partner.**

*—AC, Coach for New Leaders, Consultant*

---

It might be said that a coach is some combination of a sounding board, a truthteller, and an accountability partner. They listen attentively, challenge your thinking, call out false assumptions, and help you stay on track with the path you choose.

**COACHING CLICHÉ #2**

**A good coach does not do much work; the client does the work.**

While this is a good rule of thumb, it is also unrealistic. Coaching uses energy and takes concentration. Good coaching requires adaptability; what works for one client on one day will not be what the next client is looking for or the same client on a different day. Sometimes we ask a lot of questions. Sometimes we sit back and let the client unpack their thoughts, and then we help to reorder them.

I recently heard someone talk about the coach's burden. Although being a coach is interesting, a privilege, an opportunity, and a joy, never believe it is not a lot of work! Maintaining our coaching presence, cultivating a coaching mindset, listening actively, and asking powerful questions, all while creating a safe environment, means constantly adjusting the dials on our experience, opinions, curiosity, intrusiveness, energy, and mood. We must listen for the client's themes and ensure that we don't overlay ours. We must follow the client's agenda and make sure we don't superimpose ours. And, sometimes the most difficult of all, we must accept that sometimes we will miss a cue, ask a poor question, or highlight a theme that is not there. We are, after all, human. Fortunately, coaching is a forgiving art if we go into it with our eyes open and with good intentions. We must be forgiving too.

Another question is whether coaching is therapy. Although the answer is no, it is understandable that a client would ask the question, because so many people who have worked with a coach find it therapeutic.

Therapy is healing, curative. It fixes us in some way. Coaching does not fix us, because coaching clients are not broken. There is no pathology to remedy; if there were, we would refer the client to another professional. There is no lack to overcome; if there were, we would refer. We start with the premise that *you are enough* and that you will be able to create the solution you need. You may need additional resources, and you may need to learn new things, but you won't need to be told exactly what to do to get from here to where you want to go. Nor is it my job to tell you the best route to get there. You may enjoy the scenic route, and I might recommend toll roads. I may suggest a journey that takes a day, but you might want to take a week.

That said, it can feel like a great burden has been lifted when your coach listens with no judgment and then challenges you with a question that nudges your perspective a few degrees.

One of my favorite questions is, "What evidence do you have for that?" All of us are burdened with assumptions and unhelpful beliefs that have been instilled in us by family, friends, teachers, society, and more. All too often a coaching client will be categoric, saying things like:

"That is just the way it is."

"That is just the way I am."

"I know I can't, but I wish... ."

"I wish I could stop... ."

---

### COACHING HOLY GRAIL #2

**Our expertise is in the coaching process, not the client's life or work.**

We are comfortable not knowing the *answer* and are willing to take the steps the client needs to discover their own way forward. To this end, there is another holy grail: client context.

It does not matter what I would do, what another client would do, or what you believe the client *should* do. What matters is to help the client understand how their identity, context, environment, experiences, values, and beliefs change their experience and how their personal strengths, talents, insights, and work change the solution.

---

## The Coaching Agenda

This section could be titled "identifying where we are going and how we will know when we get there."

It may sound a bit formal and stuffy to talk about an agenda for coaching, but it is essential. Setting the agenda is often a key part of the coaching. The very process of homing in on the topic, why it is important and how the client will measure coaching success, starts to shine a light on assumptions, limiting beliefs, and unhelpful thinking. It usually starts to spark some new ideas too. It also helps the coach to understand the client, what they are looking for and why—and how they will know they have found it. The agenda is not created in stone; it can change over time. One of the roles of the coach is to check for agenda drift and help the client reset intentions, as necessary.

**COACHING HOLY GRAIL #3**

**The agenda is itself an intervention and deserves time and effort.**

The International Coaching Federation (ICF) requires coaches to work with their clients to set an agenda. There is the agenda that is the overarching purpose of the coaching engagement, and there is the agenda that we are going to focus on today. It is all too easy to skip this step and jump straight in. It is also easy to not get enough clarity in this step. What exactly will indicate success? The answer to this question is important for the coach and the client.

People show up at a coach's door for many reasons, but at the heart of most visits is the question "What is my point?"

Coaching clients arrive with various questions. Some questions might be soul-searching:

What do I want?

Where am I going?

Is this the right relationship for me?

Should I change jobs?

What next?

How do I go on?

How do I adapt?

How do I create life balance?

What is life balance?

How do I feel fulfilled?

Why do I keep making poor choices?

Who have I become?

Who do I want to become?

How do I make others listen?

What do I have to say?

What is my story?

How do I build confidence?

What is my legacy?

And some questions might be practical:

Where should I work?

Should I downsize my house?

How do I get fit? Lose weight?

How do I make a new habit stick?

How do I . . .?

As I worked on this book, an amazing group of individuals generously gave their time and thoughts to help me develop the content. One of the many questions I asked them was, "What is coaching most useful for?"

The responses from potential coaching clients are shown in this bar chart:

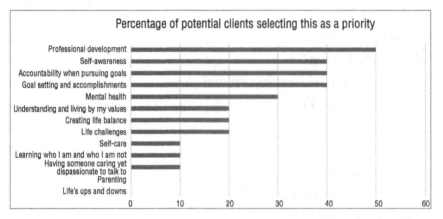

The responses from the book's advisory board are depicted in the next bar chart:

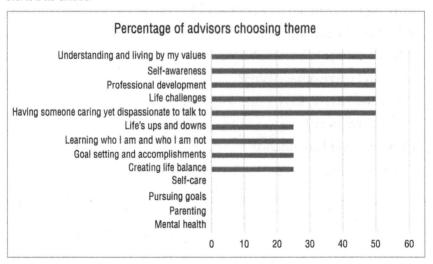

As the charts show, there is quite an overlap between clients and experts, and yet there are some striking differences. Surprisingly, our coaches did not pick "pursuing goals" as a key topic for coaching, whereas 40 percent of coaching clients did. Possibly the difference in responses comes from clients showing up with an expectation, and then finding that they want—or gain—something different from the experience, that coaching goes beyond a set of defined goals and has a broader impact (but I have not measured that hypothesis).

In my own practice I have found that a wide array of topics comes up. Often the issue or opportunity that the client arrives with is just a symptom of a broader struggle or choice. So, while the coaching client arrives seeking solutions to a problem at hand, we coaches are looking for the bigger themes. Usually these are themes that repeat themselves. Maybe the client struggles to make choices or, having made a choice, finds it hard to stick to that choice. Maybe they find it hard to resist pressure from others even though they don't want the same things.

In all of this, however, it is not the coach's role to advise. It is to encourage exploration, experimentation, and reimagination. It is to encourage the client to use what they already know about themselves to design their forward journey. We assume they know best!

---

**COACHING HOLY GRAIL #4:**

**The agenda is always the person being the person they want to be in the face of whatever is ahead of them.**

The client gets to choose the specific agenda topics that support that journey. One of the core premises in coaching is that our clients don't need us to solve the problem at hand. They come fully formed. We don't start from the premise of them having gaps, limits, or other things that must be plugged and fixed. Our abiding premise is that the client knows what they want and need; they just need to discover (or uncover) it. And they need a thinking partner to do that.

---

**COACHING CLICHÉ #3:**

**The client is their own best expert.**

Coaches often say this. The ICF even incorporates this idea into its coaching competencies and coaching ethics. While no client is an expert in everything, they are undoubtedly the best expert in their current life.

## A Sounding Board

New coaching clients are almost always curious about what other people bring to coaching, especially if they themselves are new to life, executive, or career coaching. They assume that people show up with specific goals they want to accomplish already mapped out or a mandated set of behavior modifications identified by their boss, or that they have a particular decision to make or relationship that is proving difficult.

Most clients are surprised when I tell them that about a quarter to a third of my clients use me as a sounding board. They come to talk about whatever is going on in their lives now.

Effective coaches are:

- Careful listeners
- Powerful observers
- Challenging questioners
- Theme spotters
- Solutionists
- Caring but indifferent

---

**COACHING HOLY GRAIL #5**

**Coach the client, not the problem.**

It can be difficult for any coach, but especially new coaches, to resist the urge to advise. It can seem as though there are only so many coaching problems under the sun, and when we have seen others navigate something similar, or we have seen this client go through something similar previously, the urge to lay out a solution can be overwhelming.

Even though our clients come wanting to solve today's problem, explore today's choice, or evaluate the current opportunity, our job is only partly to find the solution to *this* problem. Our real job is to reconnect who the client is with who the client wants to be—to challenge them to consider what they would do if they were being the person they want to be.

---

Although we often find ourselves listening to stories of what is going on in the moment, our mission is to remind our clients of their stated values and to explore if those values have changed; it is to remind them of their skills, strengths, preferences, and commitments. Clients may always change their minds about the purpose of coaching, about what they believe, but the coach's job is to make sure that decision is mindful, not mindless.

Hence, we will ask, "How does that decision relate to your value of. . .?" Or, "You've previously said that it is important to you to put family first; what choice is consistent with that value?"

Often the choice, solution, or decision quickly becomes clear, *or* the client discovers a new value, skill, or desire. Either way, we are helping the client decide who they will be rather than what they will do.

## A Truthteller

Another way that coaches help clients is in the relentless search for truth. Of course, everyone's version of the truth is colored by the lens through which we look at life. And that is where the coach comes in, helping you to change out the lens and consider the truth from different points of view.

How often have you dreamed a dream, imagined an outcome, or pictured yourself doing something amazing? How good are you at reality checking those dreams? Do you even want to reality check them, or do you just revel in them?

When our clients come for coaching, they have dreams and beliefs, and assumptions.

For example, they may dream of running a marathon because they assume they are too old, too unfit, and cannot do it.

They may believe that they cannot pursue their dream job because "I am just not good at math."

They may assume what is and isn't possible without checking. For example, clients often assume they know what their boss will say in response to a request. We would often rather not ride out potential disappointment and therefore don't ask for fear of what the answer will be, even though it cannot really be any worse than not answering at all.

One of my favorite quotes is generally attributed to the psychotherapist and author Virginia Satir: "People prefer the certainty of misery to the misery of uncertainty."

By asking questions about what it would take to accomplish the dream, how likely it is that the person will take those steps, what experience they have of accomplishing similarly ambitious goals, and what they already know about themselves and what they need to know, the coach can provide a check-in for the truth.

By the same token, by asking questions about assumptions, obstacles, and reasons *not* to pursue a dream, we can help clients to reach further and go beyond the boundaries of who they currently are.

One of the most common things I see in coaching is *fear*. Quite apart from our general understanding of fear, there is another factor I see at play, and fellow coaches report similar stories.

## FEAR: False Evidence Appearing Real

One of the biggest obstacles we coaches see to clients achieving their goals and finding meaning is the collection of evidence that clients use to justify their current choices.

For example:

They have been told by their parents, teachers, or friends that they are uncoordinated and don't have the stamina for a long run like a marathon.

They compare themselves unreasonably to others who run and decide that they have the wrong body shape or experience or are the wrong age.

They look at a past experience that is not closely related to the current goal and unreasonably assume that experience is a perfect predictor of future performance.

In high school I was told that I could not study for four advanced qualifications because girls don't handle that pressure as well as boys. I was also told that an advanced French qualification would not be useful for someone like me, who was "destined" to go into science and math. That was false evidence appearing real because (a) I trusted the teachers to know better than me because I was young; (b) I trusted the teachers to have my best interests at heart; (c) I assumed that science was the right subject for me to study and that my destiny was set in stone; and (d) I assumed my parents would advocate for what was best for me.

Here I am years later with two degrees in economic theory, a law degree, and training in mediation, positive psychology, and coaching. Not a scientific qualification or job in sight!

Sometimes the job of the coach is not to help the client see that they *can* achieve something they assume they cannot. Sometimes it is a sanity check in the other direction. The false evidence—other people have done it; I once ran cross-country in school; I can play racket sports, so I must be able to run; I enjoy running short distances with my dog on the beach—may be that something *is* possible that is not. Coaching can help us to avoid biases such as the availability bias—the tendency to overemphasize the most recent or most desirable result. We see it with people who start up restaurants all the time. The National Restaurant Association estimates that 60 percent of restaurants fail in their first year and 80 percent fail within 5 years. And yet year after year new restaurants open using the 20 percent success rate as an indicator of the likelihood of their own success. With coaching, a new operator would be encouraged to consider what makes the successful restaurants different from the unsuccessful ones. A coach would help a client more likely be in the 20 percent not by blind luck or good intentions but by deliberate planning.

Either way, the coach encourages the client to examine the truth. We make no judgments; we just invite reality testing.

---

**COACHING CLICHÉ #4**

**Coaches check their beliefs, preferences, and biases at the door.**

In order for this to be true, coaches would have to be completely different from everyone else. It is impossible to turn off all our biases and be completely open-minded about everything all the time. We can be:

- ■ Informed: We can explore our biases and become more aware of them.

- ■ Deliberately curious: We can ask about the client's beliefs, values, and wants and deliberately focus on what they share.

- ■ Vulnerable: We can admit when personal experience or belief is potentially getting in the way. We may even have to recuse ourselves from the coaching relationship if we find that our biases are getting in the way of our client.

- ■ Willing to consult with others: All coaches are recommended to have a coach and to have people they can consult for advice.

We don't necessarily succeed in checking biases at the door, but we do strive to know them, examine them, and take account of them in our work.

---

## An Accountability Partner

The keyword here may look like "accountability," but in many ways I believe the keyword is "partner." Although we can tag along, in the end the client decides what the work is and whether they do it. As coaches, we can check in and ask probing and powerful questions, but we cannot make changes on behalf of our client. We also cannot promise success. If the client does not want to do the work or for some reason feels unable to, we cannot do it for them.

Our greatest skill is in helping our client to decide what work needs to be done and what their motivation is for doing it. We can check in, celebrate successes, keep the client's eye on the prize, and track the progress. We can help the client regroup and adjust when things don't turn out as planned. Coaches help clients evaluate new information, realign actions with values, and even call into question—gently but firmly—the client's claims.

---

**COACHING HOLY GRAIL #6**

**Only the client gets to decide whether coaching was successful, whether they got what they wanted and/or needed.**

Coaches generally spend a lot of time thinking about their clients and considering what they, the coach, can and should explore with them. It can be tempting to try to assess our effectiveness in a coaching session. Did the client have an aha moment? Did they seem energized?

Ultimately, the client decides whether the coaching was effective. I have had many experiences where I as the coach felt that the session may have been wanting only to hear from the client that it was life-changing or that their reflection after the session had led to that aha moment.

All we can do is be present, be thoughtful, use our instincts and skills, and offer the client the best of us in the moment.

---

# Case Study: Tegan

When Tegan started to receive coaching, she was unsure of what she wanted, beyond a feeling of purpose and some inspiration to move forward.

In the first few sessions, the coach acted as a sounding board, listening closely while Tegan unpacked her concerns, disappointments, dreams, and motivations. Together, coach and client enumerated Tegan's values: community, contribution, benevolence, and self-direction. They explored Tegan's top character strengths: kindness, honesty, humor, hope, and curiosity.

They explored when and how those strengths serve Tegan well and when they might get in the way. Coach and client also explored which of the character strengths might represent cracks in the boat hull and discovered that Tegan had some quite negative views on how she engages in teamwork, leadership, and navigating uncertainty and adventure. Together, they uncovered that Tegan's lowest strength was self-investment, which meant that despite Tegan's high curiosity, she had trouble seeing the value in getting training, reading books (for learning and pleasure), and joining communities that would stimulate thinking and provide new challenges. Her focus had been very much on managing her team and on managing her children's futures.

Within two sessions, Tegan could start to see the value of coaching. Could she have achieved the same movement, insight, and change on her own? Maybe, but that was uncertain both in result and time frame. Tegan became convinced that coaching had given her a new lease on life, had reconnected her with who she was and how she wanted to be in life, and that this manifested in new habits, more energy, and a general sense that there is more to life—more hope and more fun! To Tegan, it felt like a long time since humor and playfulness had been a core part of life!

Tegan started to consider how her teamwork and leadership skills could be improved so that she could be more of a leader—a source of vision and inspiration—to her team, instead of a manager focused on tasks, timing, and performance measures.

When asked whether a coach is needed, Tegan thought long and hard before answering, "Maybe not needed like oxygen or water. Certainly, you can make do for a long time without one. But there are many things in life that we don't need minute by minute, day by day—even food. But we cannot go on forever without them and expect to thrive."

## Being a Coaching Client

> **COACHING HOLY GRAIL #7**
>
> **Coaching is *all* about the client.**
>
> What they want, what they already know, what they need to know, what resources they have, what resources they need, and where they want to go—or stay. However much the coach may envision something different or better for our client, that is not our call. If they were to succeed in our dreams, that would not feel like their own success—and if they were to fail in our dreams, whose fault would that be?

Michelle Obama once said, "Success is only meaningful and satisfying when it feels like your own."

Our curiosity is driven by what the client seeks to know, not by what intrigues us (although sometimes we get lucky and they coincide).

Our language is the language of the client enhanced by observation.

Our dreams for the client are the client's dreams.

We celebrate when the client achieves something important and meaningful to *them*, even if we would never want it for ourselves.

We bring the best of ourselves to help cultivate the best of our client—measured by them.

I mentioned at the start of this book that I am a coach bound by the ethics and standards of the International Coaching Federation. We commit to integrity, embodying a coaching mindset, and we cultivate trust and safety with our language and actions. We maintain presence and listen actively so that we can see the opportunities to evoke greater awareness in our clients. Ultimately, we aim to facilitate client growth. But these are minimum standards, and coaches have different ways to achieve them based on their training, life experience, outlook, background, and more.

Later in this book, I will offer some insights into how to be the best coaching client you can be, how to get the most out of coaching, and how to find the coach who is right for you.

For now, though, let's consider the role that hope plays in the coaching journey.

# CHAPTER 5

# Being Hopeful: *Expectation*

In every life we have some trouble, but when you worry you make it double.

—*Bobby McFerrin*

## Focusing on Hope

One of my father's favorite expressions was, "Well, that is the triumph of hope over experience!" Of course, he did not coin the phrase; that is reputed to have been Samuel Johnson. But he appropriated it—often.

Sometimes he would use it to remind us that we cannot get a different result from the same actions. Other times, it was to remind us that we are human and fallible and cannot be expected to accomplish the impossible. Most often, though, he used it to let us know that he was not a fan of our "it will turn out alright in the end" mentality.

I wish he was still around, because we would have some healthy and challenging debates about what hope is, and how it helps—especially now I have research to point to!

My mother had a different perspective. Her favorite phrase was, "It is better to travel hopefully than to arrive."

The two of them shared a philosophy of "assume the worst and hope for the best."

As I grew up, hope seemed dreamy, tantamount to wishing, and a poor foundation for anything and everything! I would not look forward to an event or occasion, because assuming the worst meant assuming disappointment—that the plans were destined to fall apart. When we drove somewhere to visit something or someone, I would love the ride, but as the remaining miles ticked down on the journey, I would start preparing myself for the inevitable disappointment of the reality of our arrival.

There are many good reasons my parents had a tentative relationship with hope, and they thought they were doing their best when they passed that on to me.

They were wrong. And my coaching clients have helped me to see that. So, I thank them for that. I now look forward to things, enjoying anticipation and excitement, safe in the knowledge that I will bounce back if I am disappointed. I no longer assume that what has happened before will happen again. I see possibilities as long as I take different action that makes my desired outcome more likely. And as I pull up to the gates of some new place or experience, I know it will not be exactly as I imagined it, and I am excited to find out what it will really be like.

That is not wishing or dreaming; it is hoping, seeing a possible future and taking steps to make it more likely to turn out that way, believing that I will have the strength and resilience to weather disappointment and come back for a new try on a new day.

## Defining Hope

Hope is the sense of what is possible and how we can make it more possible. It is not just thinking positively, dreaming of a better future, or expecting that life, the universe, or a higher power will make everything just so. In this statement, I do not mean to offend people who have spiritual and/or religious beliefs that help them navigate life. Much research shows that these beliefs are beneficial, as is the sense of belonging that joining a spiritual community offers. I want to highlight that even *with* a higher power, there are things *we* can do to get closer to our goals—just as there are actions we can take that move us further away.

One of my favorite stories is about the man who hears a radio warning about a storm coming. He decides to ride out the storm in his house, confident that his higher power will protect him. A few hours later, as the water is rising to the top of the first floor of the house, someone comes past in a rowboat and asks him to step aboard to get to higher and drier ground. He refuses. A few hours later, as he is clinging to the chimney of his house, a helicopter flies overhead. His would-be rescuer calls down to climb into a basket to be hauled into the helicopter that will take him to higher ground. He again refuses and, unsurprisingly, he drowns. Upon arrival at the entrance to the next life, he asks to speak with his higher power. When he gets the meeting, he is angry and challenges that higher power. "Why did you not save me?" he shouts.

"I sent you a radio warning, a rowing boat, and a helicopter; what more were you hoping for?" comes the answer.

Even when the higher power is on your side, it does not hurt to do what you can to make your situation better. That is *hope*.

People who are low on hope are likely to feel that life happens to them and they cannot control much about it. They are likely to feel confused and disconnected from the future. They may even feel lost. They may find it hard to picture options or think about what could be. They may not be able to connect with past exploits in a way that reinforces self-belief.

Hopeful people, however, are likely to feel that there are things they can control. They believe they can choose how to respond to the ups—and downs—of life. They see uncomfortable and difficult experiences as learning opportunities. Hopeful people are likely to be more successful academically, are likely to report feeling happier, and are likely to have a higher sense of well-being than their less-hopeful colleagues and friends.

Indeed, Viktor Frankl described the power of hope in the book *Man's Search for Meaning*. Hopeful people were realistic about their situation, believed they had a say in how they reacted to being in a concentration camp, and maintained the belief that they would navigate difficulties until they were released—whenever that might be. They did not believe blindly that they would be released by a certain date, nor that survival was even certain. They were just determined to do what they could to survive. If hope can be powerful enough to make survival more likely, what can it do for the rest of us?

In this chapter, we dig deeper into hope. In Chapter 6, "Being Strong: *Motivation*," we dig into the broader topic of character strengths—of which hope is one. Then in Chapter 7, "Being Brave: *Conversation*," we will explore bravery—yours, mine, and Jamal's. And, finally, in Chapter 8, "Being Curious: *Exploration*," we will get curious about curiosity.

## Elementary Time Travel

What does the word *hope* mean to you? Is it something akin to crossing your fingers and hoping for the best? Or is it assuming that "every little thing gonna be alright!" as Bob Marley and the Wailers told us in "Three Little Birds," even when life shows us that sometimes things are not alright?

How many times has someone asked you if something is going to happen and you have answered, "I hope so." It usually sounds like a feeling about things external to us. A wish that something would turn out a certain way. We are leaving the outcome to chance. Sometimes we even talk about blind hope or, as my father was fond of saying, the "triumph of hope over experience."

Would you be surprised to discover that hope is more than wishing? It is active. It is about setting expectations and then going after them.

Researchers such as Dr. C. R. (Rick) Snyder (1944–2006) and later Dr. Shane Lopez (1970–2016) have found that hope is multifaceted.[1,2]

First, we need a *vision* of the future—something to aim for. Then we need to be energized and motivated to make moves toward that future—we need *agency*. Finally, we need to be able to identify multiple *pathways* to follow that will get us to those goals. Some pathways will fail us, and we will need to follow a new course to our destination.

**Hope = Vision + Agency + Pathways**

Or as Snyder described it, we need willpower and way power.

If we don't have a vision, it is hard to get moving. If we don't believe we can make a difference to the outcome, that we can create pathways and actions that make that vision more likely to come true, then we will not get up and get moving. We will just wait and see—and most times be disappointed.

So, how hopeful are you? The following hope continuum may help you decide.

---

[1] S. J. Lopez, *Making Hope Happen: Create the Future You Want in Business and Life* (New York: Free Press, 2013).

[2] C. R. Snyder, *Handbook of Hope: Theory, Measures, and Applications* (San Diego: Academic Press, 2000).

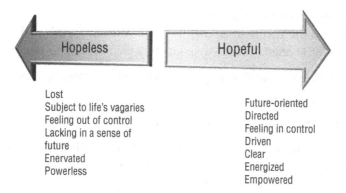

Hopeless

Lost
Subject to life's vagaries
Feeling out of control
Lacking in a sense of
future
Enervated
Powerless

Hopeful

Future-oriented
Directed
Feeling in control
Driven
Clear
Energized
Empowered

Of course, I have an assessment to recommend. The Adult Hope Scale was developed by C. R. Snyder and is considered a standard measure of hope. But I also believe we don't need a formal measure. We can use stories. Our stories. Remembering times past when we succeeded in reaching goals, picturing the future when we will reach our goals again. Hope is complicated and takes work. Most animals don't have the capacity to hope or plan because they cannot travel in time the way we do.

## A Small Amount of Brain Science

Shane Lopez, in the book *Making Hope Happen*, explains that we combine our instinctive trigger process from the amygdala to urge us to move forward, and we use our hippocampus to simulate future outcomes—to time travel. We use our rACC (rostral anterior cingulate cortex) to sort through images and ideas, selecting ones that are important and discarding ones that are not. And our prefrontal cortex allows us to do something that previous versions of humans and most animals cannot do: plan. We don't just have to wish or dream; we can create a plan that is likely to increase our chances of success.

I have a hard time remembering or even saying some of the names of the parts of the brain, but what this does tell me is that we are using an intricate process to develop hope. And I believe that each part of that process can be learned, practiced, developed, and strengthened. We can gain hope!

**Hope = Wanting to create change + Imagining possible ways to change + Sorting the best experiences of prior change + Planning the steps to change + Believing that we can weather disappointment**

Think of a goal that you have.

Look into the future and imagine that you have achieved that goal. Think about at least one possible journey or pathway to get to it.

How will you take that journey, what will you need on the way?

How do you feel?

What does reaching that goal lead to?

Now consider what steps *you* can take to make that goal more likely to come to fruition.

What will keep you motivated and energized?

How will you keep up your momentum?

Who do you need in your corner cheering you on and/or keeping you accountable?

And if your future does not come to pass as you want it to, what will you do differently? What will you learn? How will you pick yourself up and move on?

## Visualizing Outcomes

Do you know that most people are afraid of speaking in public? Even if they really know their subject matter, are well prepared, and know their audience, for many, the prospect of standing onstage and doing a striptease is less daunting than sharing their knowledge, expertise, and opinions with an audience. Some studies suggest that as many as 75 percent of people suffer from glossophobia—a fear of speaking in public. Compare that with the statistics about people who suffer from claustrophobia (fear of small spaces), which is estimated at 7 to 10 percent of the population, and we find that fear of public speaking is much more common than we might think.[3]

There are two things I want you to know at the outset:

1. Even some of the best speakers (and actors) suffer from glossophobia or "stage fright."

2. You can learn to manage it and even to enjoy public speaking!

In coaching, I and my clients have often used visualization to help picture the future and decide on a plan. Helping them to see, feel, and

---

[3] R. Black, "Glossophobia (Fear of Public Speaking): Are You Glossophobic?" *Psycom*, September 12, 2019, www.psycom.net/glossophobia-fear-of-public-speaking

even hear what is likely to happen makes the upcoming experience more real and more concrete. Visualizing not just the result but the path to get there helps them anticipate and plan mitigations for obstacles they might encounter; it focuses them on incremental progress instead of a magical result. Recollection and imagination are powerful tools in our journey to our end goal. Indeed, the brain can hardly distinguish between an experience that is imagined, remembered, or directly experienced. To the brain it is mainly the same.[4]

Many years ago, working with my own coach, I was worried about an upcoming speaking engagement. Worried is an understatement. I was *terrified*.

The speaking engagement was to be hosted online. The hosts expected anywhere from 1,000 to 2,000 people (mainly project managers) to join the call. Although the topic was something I love—character strengths—speaking publicly was new to me, although I had had the foresight to attend several Toastmasters sessions. And presenting online was new. The few presentations I had given up to that time were all in person.

As I sat with my coach bemoaning the fact that I had ever accepted the invitation to speak in the first place, she asked me to visualize the engagement.

This is the description she heard:

"I will sign on to my computer, click the link, share my screen so people can see my presentation slides, and then I will talk for an hour about strengths. Then it will be over!" I exclaimed as I imagined the relief of the presentation being finished.

The truth is that the small image of me being able to say, "I did it! It is over!" was giving me some small amount of relief. The discomfort of presenting would not go on forever, and good, bad, or indifferent, I could see that I would survive the experience.

There was a long pause, and my coach tried again.

"So, let's start at the beginning. What time will you get up?"

"Probably around 7:30 a.m.," I answered. "The presentation is at 10 a.m., but I cannot sleep in when I am nervous. I will get up, shower, choose my outfit for the day, and make some tea."

"What will the tea taste like?" my coach asked.

"Earthy," I answered. "It is black tea—English breakfast tea, my favorite blend. I don't add milk or sugar. I drink it like my father did, strong and black."

---

[4] University of Colorado at Boulder. "Your brain on imagination: It's a lot like reality, study shows." *ScienceDaily*, December 10, 2018, www.sciencedaily.com/releases/2018/12/181210144943.htm

I was getting into the swing of things now, and I continued. "I don't have much appetite when I am nervous but will have at least one slice of toast to make sure I don't feel jittery. Then I will clean my teeth, put on the outfit I have chosen, including my uncomfortable shoes that nevertheless make me feel tall and professional, and put on my makeup."

My coach asked what makeup I will wear.

In my mind's eye, I could see myself in front of the mirror, once again frustrated that I have not paid more attention to the application of makeup.

"I never wear much," I responded. "Just some mascara, foundation, face powder, and maybe some lip gloss. I have some that matches the color of my lips exactly but makes them shiny. And it tastes like strawberries." I licked my lips as I described the lip gloss. I could almost feel it on my lips as I thought about it.

Next, I described setting up my office for the call, making sure the lighting was just right, crating the dogs so they would not disturb the presentation by barking or trying to get into my office. Tidying up the pieces of paper and cardboard on the floor that my two rabbits, Dylan and BunnyPenny, have been chewing. I described setting up the desk so I could stand to present—I always feel more confident standing than sitting. I described the meditation I would do to slow my breathing and settle my nerves—alternate nostril breathing. I described the flow of my presentation, identifying when I would pause, when there would be breakouts for the audience.

As I continued to describe the session in minute detail, I could feel myself breathing more slowly and deeply. I could see and feel what it would be like to be presenting. I thought about answering questions that came up along the way and imagined myself at the start of the session inviting people to interrupt with questions as much as they wanted. (This is because if the audience holds questions to the end, it is often the case that neither I nor person asking the question can remember why it came up.) I also love interaction with the audience. I want presenting to feel like a conversation, not a monologue. We all have ideas to offer, and I am never wedded to my slides. If the audience finds a particular part of the topic fascinating, I am ready to put my slides to the side and go deeper into that.

As I continued describing the event, my confidence grew. I noted down specific comments I wanted to make, insights I wanted to make sure I shared.

By the time I had finished the visualization, it had taken me nearly 30 minutes to describe.

The clarity of the image gave it credence. I could "see" in my mind's eye the process by which I would get through the presentation. I was assured that I had done my preparation without being over rehearsed. And at the end, I remembered another of my father's pieces of advice: "Get comfortable with being uncomfortable." To him the goal was not to feel no nerves; it was to feel nervous enough to be attentive, to keep focus on the experience of the audience, and to ensure that the presenter was not complacent or smug.

"How do you feel?" asked my coach.

"Better." I answered. I had not done anything yet, but I had a clear impression in my mind of what to expect and what to aim for.

Did it turn out that way? No. But that visualization helped me feel prepared. And throughout the event, feeling prepared helped me handle the actualities of the presentation smoothly and without a sense of panic.

This is just the first step of building hope: visualizing the preferred outcome.

## Seeing Pathways

Having a clear vision of how this presentation might go was just the first step in building hope. Now I needed to think of ways that would make that outcome more likely. In this case, that involved reviewing previous work I had done on the topic of the presentation, revisiting books and TED talks from experts in the field, testing out topics on my husband and Toastmasters group, and preparing props and materials I could use during the presentation—all of which helped me make sure my learning objectives were clear and that I could deliver them effectively.

## Choosing Your Actions

One way a coach can help you is by posing what-if questions so you can imagine ways to handle various bumps and challenges that could come up. In my case, we explored everything from getting sick on the day and not being able to present, to having a smaller-than-expected audience. We worked together to anticipate possible challenges and then identify options for dealing with them. By identifying actions ahead of time, I left fewer things to chance, and again reassured myself that there are ways to deal with anything that might come up.

---

Employ realistic optimism. That is, infuse hope with probability. For example, when applying for a job you may be one of 100 applicants (low hope). If you get an interview, your chances have

increased to say one in ten (more hope). On a second interview,
your chances might be as high as one in two (lots of hope). At
each stage, you don't have certainty, but you do have increasing
chances of success.

*—Dwayne Allen Thomas, Lawyer, Writer, and Cookie Connoisseur*

What if the audience was not interested?

I had some other topics up my sleeve that I could weave into the
presentation, including some examples and some funny stories.

What if there were only a few people in the room?

I would change the style of the presentation to a group coaching
session, and we would learn together (I love group coaching, so this
was not daunting at all!).

What if I were to have an emergency, experience a power outage, or if
the Internet didn't work, or if I could not present for some other reason?

I would send them the slides and a recording before the session that
they could use if they needed to.

By the end of our three sessions, I had my vision, my pathways, and
a sense that I could do what I needed to do to make this experience OK
for me, for the audience, and the hosts.

By working with my coach on contingency planning, I felt hopeful
for the first time since agreeing to present. It was not perfect confidence,
but it was enough. Enough to help me believe it would be good enough.
Enough to help me feel that I had anticipated what could happen and
had thought out my responses. Enough felt in my control that I could
tolerate the things that were not.

## Handling Disappointment

And what if that presentation goes wrong? What then?

I pictured forgetting what I wanted to say, no one coming to the session,
people giving negative feedback, and I started to imagine how I would
learn from that experience.

If no one comes, that is probably because no one knows me—so I can
work on credibility and presence. If I forget what I want to say, I will
make it up. I know my subject, so I will improvise (I made a note to
do a crash course in improvisation which was *a lot* of fun!). And as for
feedback, I hoped it would be specific enough that I could do something
with it. It would not be a comfortable experience, but it would give me
valuable information either way.

Let's be clear, I was terrified that it would all go wrong. I did not want to experience that. But thinking about possible strategies reassured me that I would cope.

In the event, it was a washout. Nearly 2,000 people joined the online call, and instead of them each being muted, everyone's microphones were *live*. And in case you have not noticed, people join webinars from all sorts of unlikely places—their office as they discuss with HR the process for terminating a contract with someone, the bathroom where they are bathing their kids, the street, the train. Think of a noisy chaotic place, and someone is probably there.

Adding to that, the moderator got disconnected from the call, and there I was: the only one with any control over the situation at all (which was very little). I could not speak loud enough to be heard; the background noise was distracting me. This was *nothing* that I had anticipated, and yet all my preparation still helped. I knew I could not present in those circumstances, so I announced that we would be rescheduling to another day and that all the attendees would be notified of the new date (even though I was not sure we knew who all the attendees were). I ended the call and took several deep breaths.

In that moment I knew that no presentation could possibly be worse. Any presentation in the future would be at least a little better than that one. Instead of feeling beaten and hopeless, I was able to laugh and reschedule not one but two sessions with the same audience. And that was the beginning of my speaking career!

## Interactions of Hope with Other Strengths

According to character strengths research, some strengths are closely aligned with hope. If you are a high-hope individual, you are more likely to be high in zest, gratitude, perspective, perseverance, and love.

One of my favorite stories from Dr. Shane Lopez is his test of where hope comes from. In character strengths research, we think of strengths as being expressible in terms of heart and head (and internal and external relationships). Hope is believed to be slightly more heart oriented than head oriented, and more related to internal contemplation of the future. Even so, we know hopeful people tend to spread hope; it is contagious like other emotions and moods.

Dr. Lopez wanted to know from his audiences where *they* thought hope came from, so he created the Head-Heart-Holy test. He would ask everyone on the count of three to point to their heart, their head, or above them (to a higher power).

He reports several results from this casual study:

First, we don't hesitate; we each have strong convictions about where hope comes from.

Second, most people point to their heart; it is a feeling.

Third, we all look around to see where our hope community is. Where are the others who choose head, heart, or holy?

The research shows that hope is actually a very complicated process.[5]

## Case Study: Jamal

Having spent all his life in one place, Jamal has decided to go to college far from home. He wants to study abroad—in the UK. His parents are nervous for him because it will be a big change to be on his own, in a new place, at a new school with new people.

When Jamal was considering his options for making the move, he looked at local colleges, and his parents told him that they wanted him to stay at home. But as he explored his options for studying sustainability and environmental studies, Jamal realized that the best schools were not near home. They were in far-flung places such as Denmark, Sweden, and the United Kingdom.

Going abroad is daunting, but at the same time it is exciting. Jamal narrowed down his choices to Oxford and Imperial College London.

He meets with his coach to explore his options.

First, he describes his passion for sustainability and environmental science. He talks about places he has visited that still have amazing wildlife, pure water, and clean air. He describes how that compares with life in cities. He explains that he has created various recycling and reuse experiments at home, using rainwater to irrigate their vegetable garden, experimenting with different vegetable crops to see what grows best.

Next, he explains that he wants to go to the best school he can, but does not want to upset his parents. He is nervous about the big change that going away to school will mean for him. The people Jamal grew up with are all going to a local two-year college. Some of them are even going to be studying together. It feels uncomfortable to not be part of the crowd.

---

[5] S. J. Lopez, *Making Hope Happen: Create the Future You Want in Business and Life* (New York: Free Press), 21.

Jamal's coach asks him what he wants. After thinking about it for a minute, Jamal comes up with this list:

1. I want to be an environmental scientist.

2. I want to make a difference to the planet, to everything that lives here; I want to reduce forest fires, droughts, and other symptoms of global warming.

3. I want to travel and see the perspectives of people outside this country.

4. I want to take on new challenges, see new things, and show myself and my parents that I can manage even if things feel strange and uncomfortable.

Next his coach asks him to visualize what the future will look like. "Imagine your life turns out exactly as you want, it is 10 years from now, what does that life look like, how do you feel in that life?" She encourages him to consider all his senses as he projects forward to who he will be in 5 or 10 years' time.

Jamal closes his eyes, picturing that life. His breathing slows, he smiles slightly.

Jamal starts to describe his future story. "I travel 10 months of the year; I am attending meetings, symposia, conferences, government forums, advising on the changes we need to make to save the planet. I am invited to speak all over the world, and to visit remote places to examine what is happening to the world. I am working with a team of international scientists and influencers who are creating a worldwide plan to halt and maybe even reverse global warming. It is collaborative. We have created a worldwide foundation, and the world is finally acting on global warming.

"I see myself shaking hands, meeting powerful people in the private sector and in national governments. I am a spokesperson for the movement. My superpower is taking the complex science and boiling it down into understandable chunks of information. I use my studies to inform my speaking, but I am no longer just a scientist. I am an influencer.

"My parents are proud. They feel that I am making a difference, that I am competent and respected. They are retired and often travel with me to places they have never seen."

Jamal is smiling, pleased with his vision of the future. Now it is time to create pathways and take action to make as much of this dream come true as possible.

When his coach asks Jamal how likely these outcomes are, Jamal looks puzzled. How could he know? All these things were just wishes, right?

Next his coach asks what steps he has in mind to make each of these outcomes more likely. She asks him to explore all the different ways he might reach his goal, and to consider which of those he is most likely to be able to influence.

Having created a vision, Jamal is moving on to considering pathways and agency.

## Cultivating Hope

Hope takes practice. Some of us are naturally more hopeful than others, but all of us can learn to be *more* hopeful. By working on developing a clear vision of our possible future, we can "see" it more clearly and pursue it as a goal.

By practicing identifying pathways to that future—even ones that seem unlikely to succeed—we generate options. We can do this at any time, even for simple tasks. For example, when going somewhere we often visit, we can practice identifying new routes.

And by thinking specifically about what we can and will do to make the outcome more likely, we build confidence and self-belief.

The more we do these things, the more hopeful we become and the less work being hopeful seems to take.

## Case Study: Jamal

Jamal has a clear vision of his ideal future, but so far has not really explored what it will take to get there.

For example, the move to a new location. How will he stay motivated to make the move as the time approaches? How will he overcome loneliness? How will he handle being uncomfortable in a new place? What can he do ahead of the move to prepare?

Jamal decides to use social media to make connections in London and Oxford so that he can get to know people before his first visit. He also researches different locations to live and what travel will look like. He quickly establishes that a car will be too expensive, so he will need to live close enough to school to take public transportation. He starts to learn all the subways (the Underground) routes in London and learns the layout of Oxford. After several weeks of studying the Internet, maps, and books, he knows where all the different colleges are in Oxford, and he has identified three areas in London and two more in Oxford that he will consider for living.

Seeing that he is doing a lot of work to make his dream a reality, Jamal's grandmother offers to pay for him to fly to the UK to visit London and Oxford, and he gladly takes her up on her offer. He has been saving money, so he decides to use that to pay for accommodation and travel while he is there—including taking the train from London to Oxford to visit the town.

## Hope Is Not Just for Individuals

A few years ago, I was able to conduct a study on project managers. I was using an assessment to determine whether there were character strengths that are more common in project managers than in other people. The early findings seemed to suggest that project managers are higher in hope than other people. This makes sense: How do you get to the end of a project, with all its ups and downs, without a vision of the future and a belief that you and the team can build a plan and take steps to make that future a reality?

According to character strengths research, hope is closely linked to other character strengths such as perseverance, perspective, gratitude, zest (enthusiasm), and love.[6]

And we also know that hope, along with curiosity, love, zest, and gratitude, is correlated with higher levels of well-being and life-satisfaction. Hope, gratitude, curiosity, love, and zest lead us to a great sense of meaning!

There is limited research into the role of hope in the workplace, but at least one study has shown that teams with high hope were more successful in facing and overcoming challenges. One of the reasons, the researchers found, was that there is an emotional contagion effect.[7] So, when you cultivate your own hope, you may indirectly be lifting the spirits and hopefulness of others around you.

---

[6] R. M. Niemiec, *Character Strengths Interventions: A Field Guide for Practitioners* (Boston: Hogrefe Publishing, 2018).
[7] K. B. Sawyer and J. A. Clair, "Hope Cultures in Organizations: Tackling the Grand Challenge of Commercial Sex Exploitation," *Administrative Science Quarterly* 67, no. 2 (2022): 289–338, https://doi.org/10.1177/00018392211055506

This contagion effect was very apparent when I was perusing the Internet and saw this quote from Anoop Prasad, Advocacy Director of the Asian Prisoner Support Committee:

> When you talk to someone who has been down for decades and still has fight in them, you do not get to give up. So, I fight alongside you and hope alongside you—even when it seems impossible. I carry your hope inside of me out of those prison walls. What you may not realize is that your hope is contagious.

## YOUR HOPE FOR THE FUTURE: REFLECTION QUESTIONS FOR *YOU* TO PONDER

Here are some questions for you to consider as you work on building your own levels of hope:

- ▪ What is something that you want to accomplish in the next month?
- ▪ When you have accomplished this, what will life be like? How will you feel? How will your senses be stimulated? What will have changed in your life?
- ▪ What are three different ways that you could move toward that goal? Who might you talk to? Where might you go? Who can help?
- ▪ What are three actions you will take in the next week to move toward your goal? How will you feel when you complete those actions?
- ▪ How do you feel?

# Being Strong: *Motivation*

A woman is like a tea bag. You can't tell how strong she is until you put her in hot water.

—*Eleanor Roosevelt*

## Strengths as Pathways to Motivation

Working on this chapter has once again encouraged me to pause and contemplate character strengths. Mine, yours, everyone's.

My top strengths are appreciation of beauty and excellence, bravery, curiosity, fairness, and gratitude. Each of those strengths feels like it is at my fingertips or on the tip of my tongue. And these strengths together create a bias in me. They mean I look for the best in people and find it easy to see strengths even in difficult people. I speak out and speak up even when it is uncomfortable. I share things others may not. I am always asking questions and looking for new ways to interpret things. I want others to have the same chances, and I want them to have access to the resources they need, and I am grateful for all the opportunities I have had to learn, live and, above all, to experiment. Even when life is challenging and difficult, I am grateful nonetheless.

As I started this chapter, I found myself wondering what other strengths I need to focus on at this time. We don't show up one strength at a time; instead, we are a constellation of strengths. And as natural as some strengths feel, we can always cultivate others. I have a deck of strength cards, and I shuffled them and picked one at random. The first card I picked was social intelligence.

Social intelligence is the strength most associated with understanding—of ourselves and others. It is about seeing, hearing, and feeling what motivates us and the people around us. It is about adaptability, making space for others, and really paying attention to what is said—and not said. What an apt strength for this chapter. *My* motivation is always to help, teach, share knowledge, empower, encourage, to offer resources, and to create a safe environment where you can experiment too. But what of my reader's motivation? Most people pick up a book like this in search of a solution to a life problem, or they are looking for insights into how and why they feel as they do. Or maybe it is to get a better understanding of how someone you know may be benefiting (or not) from a coaching relationship. Whatever your reason for being a reader of this book, you have a question to answer, a problem to solve, or some knowledge to glean. Welcome.

So, as I write this chapter, I want to remember that whatever *my* motivation for being here, I want to help you get closer to satisfying *your* motivation for being here. I will do my best to make this chapter—and all the others—about you, and what you might be looking for and not just about what I want to talk about!

## Character Strengths 101

I first encountered character strengths and the science of character in a course about positive psychology. The Certificate in Positive Psychology explored many aspects of this young science. Sometimes called "the science of peak performance" or "the science of flourishing," the many tools of positive psychology each have their place in the helping professions, and in coaching. From growth mindset to cultivating courage, from neuroplasticity to the influence of language on our thinking, the field grabbed my attention. But no topic made as big an impression on me as character strengths.

Simply put, *character strengths* are the positive parts of our personality—the parts of us that give us the potential to be great. And they can also get in our way. When we know and show our character strengths, and invite in the strengths of others, collaboration and innovation soar (as long as our strengths don't go overboard).

Strengths and their appropriateness are contextual, and as we learn about our strengths, we want to be able to turn up—and turn down—the dial on them depending on where we are and who we are with. My curiosity can be great in a room full of outgoing people too nervous to get to know each other, but it can feel like the Spanish Inquisition to someone who is reserved and shy.

## Strengths-Spotting in Coaching

One of the best tools that coaches have is strengths-spotting. Of course, we can use any of several assessments to measure our character strengths. My personal favorite is the assessment from the VIA Institute on Character in Cincinnati because the basic assessment is free. But there are many more assessments that work well. I find it especially helpful to use an assessment when coaching in groups because it gives a framework and language with which we can all work. It makes it simple to look at the group culture as measured by the character strengths that show up.[1]

But just as powerful as an assessment is, strengths-spotting from the stories that our clients tell is at least as, if not more, effective. Being able to notice and describe strengths in a client's story is a very potent coaching intervention. And the language does not matter. In fact, it can be part of the coach-client bond to use descriptions that are personally meaningful to them even if they would not mean much to someone else. For example, a coaching client refers to *Heat culture* when he wants to remind himself about being determined, hardworking, collaborative, and putting the needs of the team ahead of personal needs. It is a shorthand that he and I understand.

Some research has suggested that two-thirds of us are strengths-blind. That is, we don't recognize our special qualities as strengths; we just assume they are "common." Our focus tends to be on our gaps and deficits. We may forget to celebrate—and leverage—our strengths.

---

[1] I wrote a book about character strengths in project management that was published in 2018 by Berrett-Koehler Publishing. *Be a Project Motivator, Unlock the Secrets of Strengths-Based Project Management* is still available and is the basis for a LinkedIn Learning course called Project Manager to Project Motivator.

And a coach who is on the lookout and is comfortable spotting strengths in their clients helps to build self-esteem, confidence, and a more balanced view of what the client has to offer the world.[2]

So, I am always on the lookout for strengths. Not just in coaching conversations—although that is a critical part of my practice—but in general and casual conversations, in line at the supermarket, or when getting coffee in the local coffee shop. Being able to see a behavior, name it, and describe the strengths behind it is very empowering for the person I am talking to, and for me! And, as I often tell audiences at conferences, no one has ever complained about my strengths-spotting. I almost always get one of these responses:

- "Wow, you saw that in me? People don't often say that about me."
- "Thank you. I think that is a core part of who I am."
- "You see that as a strength? I have never thought of it that way before."
- "I just did what anyone would do." (More on this in Chapter 7, "Being Brave: *Conversation*.")

I find that when a coaching client has something they want to accomplish, tapping into their strengths is a great first step to progress because it ties that goal to what motivates, energizes, and excites them most.

## Character Strengths as Core Motivators

> Knowing what I am really good at helps me to offer that to others. Knowing what I am not good at helps me to seek it out in others. No one has everything he/she needs. We need to build a team with diversity of strengths.
>
> —*Jana Wardian, Assistant Professor for Research, managing research and quality improvement projects*

Early in my career as a coach, I discovered the impact that strengths-spotting can have—on clients, colleagues, friends, family members, and even on complete strangers.

---

[2] Linley, A., *Average to A+: Realising Strengths in Yourself and Others* (Coventry, UK: CAPP Press, 2008).

There are several types of strengths as depicted here:

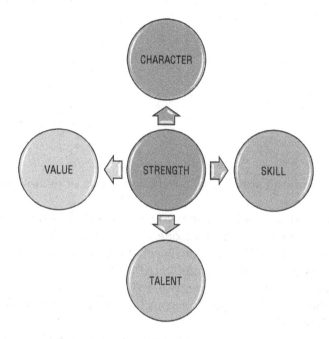

First there are talents—those things we seem naturally able to do. For example, some people have great hand-eye coordination, others can quickly learn new languages, some have a musical talent. Some are good at mathematics or visualizing abstract ideas.

Then there are skills. These are often talents that have been honed and trained and refined, but they can also be skills that have little to do with natural talents.

We also have values—those beliefs and principles that guide our lives and that influence our choices and decision-making.

All these strengths are important and have a significant impact on the quality and direction of our lives. But the last 20 years have been ones of great discovery in another area: character strengths.

## Some Thoughts About Motivation

How motivated are you? What motivates you?

Of course, the answer to these questions depends on the topic at hand. Personally, I am not motivated at all to go to the dentist even though I know I should, but I am very motivated to write this book.

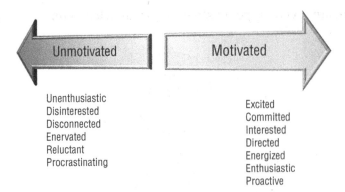

This continuum shows some of the indicators of demotivation and motivation.

Think of an area of life where you are expected or required to act, deliver something, care for someone, or get something done.

How would you describe your level of motivation on a scale of 1 to 10 (1 not motivated, 10 very motivated). What is one word you could use to describe your level of motivation?

Now think of other aspects of your life. What is your level of motivation for them?

Motivation is often discussed in terms of *extrinsic motivation*—things that come from outside us, such as money, prestige, and recognition. But there is also *intrinsic motivation*—the motivation that comes from inside us, due to our values, beliefs, and . . . strengths of character.

All types of motivation have their place, and most of my coaching clients describe motivation as coming from multiple sources—or at least the most robust motivation does because that makes it resilient. If your salary is not feeling like much of an incentive today, but your sense of teamwork and connection to your colleagues feels good, you remain motivated.

## Case Study: Tegan

Today Tegan's coach is contemplating strengths-spotting.[3] Once Tegan has set the agenda for the day, identified measures of success, and checked in and updated the coach with latest developments and accomplishments, it is time to dig into the session.

---

[3] To find out more about strengths-based practice, see: R. M. Niemiec and R. Pearce, "The Practice of Character Strengths: Unifying Definitions, Principles, and Exploration of What's Soaring, Emerging, and Ripe With Potential in Science and in Practice," *Frontiers in Psychology*, 2020, https://doi.org/10.3389/fpsyg.2020.590220

By this time, they are already nearly 20 minutes into their coaching session. Having just sorted through all that has happened and what they are going to explore for the day, Tegan comments, "I already feel clearer!" Good coaches take time with the agenda and the introduction. This is one of their strengths: allowing the right amount of time for clients to get where they need to be.

A colleague I peer coach with has this lovely practice of starting the session by asking, "How are you feeling? What do you need to be ready for our session?"

I love these two questions. Some days I don't need anything; I am feeling ready, my purpose for the session clear. On other days, I need a moment of silence and reflection. This opening feels spacious, welcoming, and made to measure. The best sessions generally don't start in a rush.

Tegan's agenda for the day is to identify some specific actions to help her plan a transition to something new and meaningful in her professional life.

The coach invites Tegan to tell a story of a time when she previously navigated a similar big life transition. Tegan thinks deeply and then tells this story.

"I was in high school. My parents had grand plans for me to go to university. They were the first in their families to do so, and their ambition was for me to go to a top-notch school as a natural progression for the family. My teachers agreed with my parents, and together my teachers and parents came up with a list of potential schools. Top of the list were Oxford and Cambridge in the UK To get into these schools required a special course of study, taking an entrance examination, and then going for interviews at the schools.

"I had *no* interest in going to either school. I had some strong (negative) biases about those schools and some definite stereotypes about what the people who go to those schools are like. I realize now that, had I been more curious, I might have discovered something different, but at the time, my focus was on making my mark my way.

"I tried to persuade my parents and teachers alike that going to one of those schools was not my ambition or my desire—but my perspective was generally dismissed as being immature and not knowing what was best for me. Feeling I had lost the battle but maybe not the *war*, I went through the motions. I showed up in the classes but sat at the back and read books. And when it came time to take the examination, I filled in my name, the date, and stopped there. I did not write another word. Saying this out loud, it all sounds very passive-aggressive, even weak, but I was 17 and did not know the things I know now. Nor was I the person I am now!

"I told my parents what I had done. They were disappointed—even furious. An eerie tense silence settled over the house. The headmistress called to discuss my 'behavior' with my parents, saying that I had embarrassed the school and potentially made it harder for other girls to be taken seriously in the future. Then a few days later, much to my surprise I got a letter from one of the colleges in Oxford inviting me for an interview. Apparently, this college within the Oxford system did not rate the exams all that highly and had a policy of interviewing everyone who applied!

"My parents were thrilled, and this was an opportunity for me to redeem myself. I went to Oxford the night before my interview (I was applying to study mathematics), and as I sat with the other interviewees, I overheard a group of them talking about the math questions they had been asked to solve in the interview. I listened—not for a moment thinking I would get the same questions—but just curious to understand the type of questions that came up in the interview.

"The next morning, I sat in the interview and . . . you guessed it, was asked the same questions as the group had been discussing the night before. I explained to the interviewers that I had already known those questions—and they said it did not matter. After the interview was over, I went to the school office and explained to the bursar that I had, at least in my mind, 'cheated.' He assured me I had done no such thing and said, 'The interviewers are looking for how you solve the problem, not whether you get the right answer.'

"I thanked him for his time, explained that I did not really want to come to Oxford—that it was a dream of my parents—and apologized for having wasted the time of all involved.

"'This place is not for everyone,' he replied, 'but may I suggest that you don't rush to a decision?'

"Funnily enough, although that visit was full of stress and pressure, I remember how bright and sunny the weather was and how beautiful the old buildings looked in the sunshine. The weather was mild but not too hot, there was a damp smell in the air like when it had just rained, and I could hear birds and bees. Despite being anxious, I felt excited to be taking on the adults to get what I thought was best.

"I was offered a place at that college, which I turned down in favor of going to another university where I studied economics, and the rest, as they say, is history."

Throughout the story, the coach has been sitting still, listening intently, only occasionally taking a few notes. As Tegan wraps up, the coach pauses, finishing off a few notes, and then asks, "Is it OK that I share with you what I heard in that story?"

Tegan agrees enthusiastically, and the coach hands over a sheet of paper.

- Willing to take risks and ride out storms

- Integrity/authenticity

- Honorable

- Strong sense of self-determination

- Always looking for ways to overcome obstacles that seem insurmountable

- Creative

- An actress

- Steady and patient; perseverant

- Brave and tolerant of discomfort

- Able to manage emotions and decisions

- Gratitude

- Appreciation of things outside you

- You were not willing to accede to the wishes of others, however well meaning.

- You were true to what you wanted and believed.

- Despite deceiving your parents, you were painfully honest with the school.

- You knew what you wanted and didn't want.

- You didn't give in when the first approaches did not yield the outcome you wanted.

- You were able to put on an act for others in support of your goals.

- You did not rush from one solution to another but played out the game to your own ends.

- Knowing that your parents and teachers would be disappointed and maybe even hurt or embarrassed, you were able to tolerate those uncomfortable feelings.

- You did not get emotional or argumentative but relentlessly pursued your goal.

- You succeeded.

- You recognized that this was an opportunity others would want even if you did not.

- Despite the stress, you noticed the weather, the aromas, and the sounds around you.

Tegan's coach has also jotted down some strengths to explore further—such as fairness, love of learning, hope, humility, love, perspective, social intelligence, teamwork, self-compassion, kindness to others, self-belief, and self-confidence.

Before we discover what Tegan thought about the feedback, and how Tegan and the coach used these observations to plan Tegan's next steps, let's reflect for a moment on what the coach was able to do for Tegan.

First, by asking about a prior experience, the coach can get Tegan to connect not just to the thoughts about what happened and what she did at that time in her life but also experience some of the feelings she had at that time. She is reminded of things she has accomplished in the past, even before she "was who she is now and knows what she knows now." She reconnects to what she was willing to do to accomplish the outcome she wanted.

And Tegan can start building her own plan based on what she already knows about herself. The coach does not need to solve the specific problem Tegan is here with: creating a sense of meaning and direction for her life. She only needs to get Tegan thinking for herself *and* becoming more aware of what tools she has in her personal toolbox.

Coaches are always partnering with their clients. Unlike consulting and mentoring, where there is generally a power differential in favor of the consultant or mentor, in coaching the coach is the expert in coaching and the clients are the experts in their own lives!

## Assessments vs. Storytelling

So why not use an assessment to evaluate Tegan's strengths? We have already discussed the use of assessments in an earlier chapter, and in some circumstances, where there is a specific need for common strengths language, or there is a group or team involved, a lot of positive things can be said for using an assessment.

As you can see from this story, though, the power of storytelling is real. Tegan is directly engaged in selecting what parts of her story to focus on, and the coach is in observer mode, just looking for strengths to highlight and describe. The way the coach describes the strengths may coincide with the standard language of an assessment, or the coach may just describe the behavior he or she sees.

And when clients see or hear about those strengths, they know something about their story shone a light on the strengths the coach observed.

Assessments can be helpful when individuals are struggling to identify a story of themselves in a related situation, or where the coach is finding it hard to spot strengths. But an assessment, to me, is always second choice for an individual, because nothing beats your own story!

In groups, strengths-spotting is powerful, even if you start off with an assessment. The more people can listen for and articulate the strengths they hear in what people tell them, the easier it is to communicate and to see value in each other.

Tegan's coach is quite comfortable in strengths-spotting. She also recognizes that one story may not highlight all the strengths that Tegan has at her fingertips. She is aware that some of her own strengths' descriptions may need adjusting for them to be truly meaningful to Tegan. But this process of strengths-spotting is also building their rapport and trust.

## Case Study: Tegan

Tegan takes a few moments to review the notes from the coach before her coach asks, "How does it feel to read those thoughts?"

Tegan is smiling and yet a little damp-eyed. She explains that she tends to think of that story as being full of examples of how she was selfish and put her own desires before those of her parents. She has not really thought of it as an example of her showing strengths.

As she looks through the list of strengths and the examples, she says, "I am not sure how to align honor, authenticity, and integrity with lying to my parents."

The coach pauses while Tegan thinks. Then Tegan says, "At the time, as a 17-year-old, it felt as though I had very little leverage to persuade people of what I wanted and they did not.

"Thinking back on that experience, I am grateful, because it showed what I could do if I set my mind to it. And it was the first time I did anything to contradict my parents. I know I was terrified—as if they would cast me out"—Tegan chuckles—"but I also believed that the alternative would turn me into a resentful person who would never achieve much, and I did not want that. I was confident that my parents ultimately did not want that. If they saw me now, they would be surprised at what I have done, where I have been, and the things I have learned!"

The coach asks another question: "What would you change about the observations I shared?"

"Well," says Tegan, "I want to dig into that bravery strength. I am not sure that I see that. I would have said 'cantankerous' or 'capricious'." She laughs again.

"Although I do love that you said I am tolerant of discomfort and patient and perseverant, I don't tend to think of myself that way. But now you have pointed it out, I can see it more clearly. That will help me as I move forward.

"I also love that you called out appreciation—I do feel that one of my strengths is to be able to see things from different angles, to be able to appreciate good things even when I am confronted with tough things. I remember when my father died suddenly. I was struck by the irony that after we had all assumed that Dad would be around to annoy us forever, he died young doing something he loved—eating! Even though I was desperately sad, he also made me laugh.

"Before today I might have called that perspective, but appreciation is a good description too because it is about making the time and space to notice what else is around me beyond whatever is consuming my attention for now.

"One of the things this story did not really highlight is my deep love of learning and relentless curiosity. In this story, it sounds as though learning is not up there as a high strength for me, but I think it showed up in my curiosity to work out how to answer the interview questions that the other students were discussing—not because I thought it would give me an advantage in the interview, but just because it was a puzzle to solve."

Tegan decides to reflect further on the story and before the next coaching session to identify things she can learn from their work today that will help her as she designs the next phase of her life.

## Knowing Your Strengths

What is the advantage of being able to identify your strengths?

> If we want to move forward in anything, I believe we should understand and leverage our strengths. By identifying our uniqueness and being OK with it, we open up a world of possibilities.
>
> —*Dorisse Shakir-Ullah, Career Strategist and Facilitator*

And how does it help to be able to see your own actions and choices as both strengths and opportunities for change? For example, when Tegan talks about her story as "selfish," there may be great things to learn. At the same time, when the coach highlights some of the strengths in the story, this invites Tegan to look at the behaviors from a different perspective. This 360-degree view of what we do and who we are is part of the power of coaching. There are always multiple ways of looking at the same thing.

Here are some of the things that have been discovered over the years by different researchers:

- People who know their strengths are nine times more engaged at work.[4]

- People who know and deliberately use their strengths at work are 18 times more engaged.[5]

- People who know and use their strengths and are encouraged to use their strengths by their leaders and managers are 29 times more likely to be engaged at work.[6]

---

[4] L. C. Hone, A. Jarden, S. Duncan, and G. M. Schofield, "Flourishing in New Zealand Workers: Associations With Lifestyle Behaviors, Physical Health, Psychosocial, and Work-Related Indicators," *Journal of Occupational and Environmental Medicine* 57, no. 9 (2015): 973–983.
[5] Ibid.
[6] Ibid.

- The Gallup organization has been tracking engagement for years and has found that people who use their strengths are more engaged, are more likely to stay in their jobs, and are more productive and cause fewer errors/safety issues.

- Gallup also identified that by focusing on the strengths of their team members, managers make a bigger difference than any other single factor on the engagement of team members.

- Studies of personal relationships have shown that awareness and appreciation of a partner's strengths increases relationship satisfaction and commitment.[7]

Many more studies and findings show that strengths of any kind are worth knowing and cultivating.

So how can you discover your strengths?

Here are some options:

1. Record or write a story about when you were at your best (as Tegan did). Put the story away for a couple of days, and then reread it / listen to it and highlight the strengths you see. Don't worry about the language; just describe what you read and hear.

2. Find someone you trust—or work with a coach—and tell a story of when you were at your best and ask that person to listen for strengths and name and describe them for you. They are looking for behavior that makes them think of something they consider to be a strength. Another option is to join a group coaching program that uses a strengths approach.

3. Take an assessment. As previously mentioned, I like the VIA Institute on Character's assessment. The basic assessment is free. You receive your ranking of 24 strengths as soon as you complete the assessment. There are more in-depth personalized reports available as well such as one that combines character strengths with five facets of mindfulness. However, there are many other assessments to get you started. Check with your HR department to see if there is one that they recommend (and might pay for).

But knowing, showing, and growing your character strengths is only half the story. It gets you a long way, but you can go further!

---

[7] T. B. Kashdan, D. V. Blalock, K. C. Young, K. A. Machell, S. S. Monfort, P. E. McKnight, and P. Ferssizidis (2017). Personality strengths in romantic relationships: Measuring perceptions of benefits and costs and their impact on personal and relational well-being. *Psychological Assessment.* http://doi.org/10.1037/pas0000464

# What Else Do You Need to Know About Strengths?

In addition to the great qualities and opportunities that strengths offer, there can be pitfalls too.

For example, how are you over- or underusing a strength?

What do you know about how your strengths affect other people around you?

When does your strength use cause you and others a cost?

## The Golden Mean

Plato, the Greek philosopher, is credited with coining the phrase the *golden mean*. It is also sometimes known as the *golden middle way*.

It is that point where there is not too much nor too little. There is just enough of a virtue, or in this case a strength.

Getting it just right means considering context, the sensibilities of other people, cultural norms, customs, traditions, and more.

For example, my top strengths are:

- **Appreciation of beauty and excellence**—In my case, a deep appreciation and even excitement about trees, birds, bees, elephants, butterflies, blue sky, water, in fact everything in nature. I also appreciate exhibitions of skill, such as a wonderful pianist, or orchestra, painter, or scientist.

- **Bravery**—The ability to tolerate discomfort and to push through difficult situations.

- **Curiosity**—Wanting to know more about everything, or as I sometimes call it "shiny new thing" syndrome.

- **Fairness**—Wanting everyone to have the same experience, creating consistent experiences for all.

- **Gratitude**—Being grateful for opportunities, the things we have, focusing on what there is and not what is missing.

These are my top strengths. They are not my only strengths, but they *are* my go-to strengths. I use them almost without thinking, and that is where the trouble sometimes starts. Any of these strengths can contribute to excessive or unpopular behavior, but the two strengths that can get me in the most trouble are bravery and curiosity. While it is good to be tolerant of discomfort, uncertainty, and fear, not every discomfort can be justified. Sometimes brave is just plain reckless.

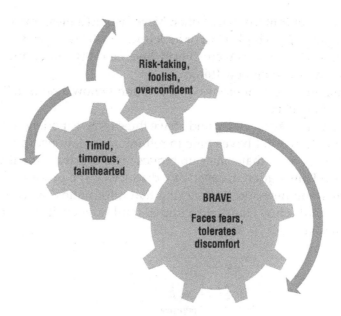

This diagram shows underuse (top left), overuse (top right) and optimal use (bottom right) of bravery.

For example, when I first started speaking in public, I would share some very personal information. It was usually well received and helped people to feel a more personal connection to me. I would share my experiences of lifelong struggles with anxiety and explain that my father suffered from obsessive-compulsive disorder (OCD) and my mother was a depressive. While I don't regret the sharing that I did so early on, I also recognize that I did it without much consideration for possible consequences. For example, the first time my anxiety and how it might affect my work came up in an interview, I was shocked. But the interviewer had been at the same conference as me. When clients explore with me what to reveal at work about their own mental health experiences, every fiber in my being screams *share*. How are we going to remove stigma and make workplaces safe for everyone if we don't speak up and challenge norms?

But that is not my job as a coach to decide for you. Nor is it necessarily the best decision for you. You know best what is brave and what is reckless in the context of your life. We work together to find out what the priority is for you, to consider the benefits and disadvantages of whatever options are available. We look at things from different perspectives to help coaching clients reach the right decision for them in this situation. The decision might look different for someone else, or even for the same person on a different day.

Similarly, curiosity is my friend, and for a long time I thought there was no such thing as too much curiosity. Practically everything interests me;

I inherited that trait from my father. Never would a meal go by without him jumping up to check a fact or look up a word. I was fortunate to live in a house where books were everywhere, and my father and mother were always learning new things.

The mantra in our house was, "If you don't know, find out. If you do know, double-check!"

As the years have gone by, and I have three times experienced burnout in relation to work, I have come to rethink my relationship with curiosity. If every topic that comes up piques my curiosity and I always act on it, then I am scattered, constantly distracted. The process of finding out something new and then storing that information away is energy sapping. Suddenly, I started to understand how curiosity may have killed the cat!

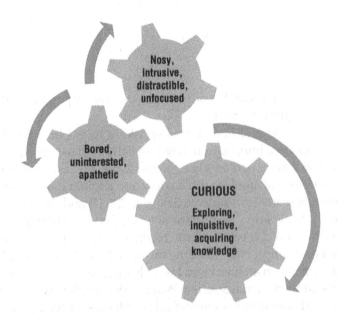

This diagram shows underuse (top left), overuse (top right) and optimal use (bottom right) of curiosity.

My personal experience of curiosity is that it is fickle and that satisfying my curiosity can get in the way of being focused and getting things done, even things that are my stated priorities. When I am researching for this book, for example, I can find myself down a rabbit hole—or more like a rabbit warren—of tangentially related material that is fascinating but not getting the book developed. And that, for now, is a *huge* priority.

To reach that golden mean, I call on other strengths to create balance.

Before we go further, pause a moment and think about your top strengths. In what ways do they make life better?

In what ways do they sometimes get in the way?

And what actions can you take and which strengths and habits can you engage to bring your strengths back to their golden mean?

## The Art of Balancing

One of the biggest revelations for me in coaching was when I realized that balance is not static. That may sound obvious, but the realization that balance is dynamic—what feels balanced today may feel unbalanced tomorrow—changed my coaching. One person's balance is another's out of control.

Often coaching clients, including me back in the day, arrive in coaching looking for the recipe for balance. In fact, coaching clients are often looking for the recipe for lots of things: relationships, work, family, self, and more. What we discover is that there is no recipe, or if there is, it needs adjusting from time to time—a little sweeter in one situation and a little thinner in another.

As a friend of mine said, "Balance is the dynamic tension between multiple ways to fall over!"

To create the golden mean with my own strengths, I use a wide array of other strengths, even ones that don't come very naturally to me.

When curiosity is taking over, I use self-regulation, meditation, lists, plans, and friends who know what my goals are to help me stay on track and keep distractions to a minimum. This combination of my own strengths and the strengths of others makes it more likely that my level of curiosity will be just right.

When it comes to bravery, it is often exacerbated by zest. My enthusiasm for helping others, solving problems, fixing things, and generally sharing whatever I have with other people makes me inclined to agree to things before taking into account the effort and potential opportunity cost of saying yes. Recognizing this, I realized I needed to have a process in place to force a pause and to consider all aspects of a request before saying yes.

For example, when I am asked to take on a speaking engagement, it is important that I check to see what else I am committed to at around the same time. Experience tells me that I cannot speak, coach, and travel all in the same day. I cannot coach more than four people in a day and expect to be effective and present. I cannot do more than four to five hours of speaking in a day before I lose focus. And it does not work for me to do back-to-back training days. If I train all day one day,

I need to take a break and do something entirely different the next day to recuperate.

When I attend conferences, I know to pace myself, which generally includes *not* meeting lots of people for dinners in the evening. I need downtime and mind off time if I am going to make it through the entire conference.

To help me take more time to reflect when being asked to an event, I created a checklist. It reminds me of my priorities and helps me decide how the latest opportunity aligns with my priorities. (See Appendix E, "Is It Time for a Change? Is This a Coaching Moment for You?" for a sample of the questionnaire.)

I can always override the results of my thoughtful assessment, but at least the process helps me to create space, think carefully, dial back impetuousness, and really think about the cost of saying yes. To me, this is me using a plan to counteract my zest for things I am asked to do. It is balancing kindness to me with kindness to others. It is also reminding me that to be kind to one audience, I may need to say no to another audience. I am, like you, a finite resource.

It is also important to me to model behavior that is as healthy as possible. Making rushed decisions and overextending myself are likely to impact the quality of my coaching *and* normalize overcommitting.

And one of the side pleasures of these behaviors is that people often see strengths in me that are *not* my top strengths, because I am dialing them up to balance my go-to strengths.

## SEAing Is Believing

One of my favorite interventions that I share in workshops, presentations, and group coaching programs is the SEA method, which was shared with me by Dr. Ryan Niemiec, Chief Science and Education Officer at the VIA Institute on Character.

SEA stands for:

- **Spot/See**—Wherever you are, whatever you are doing, look out for behaviors in others that seem like positive traits or what we are calling *character strengths*.

- **Explain**—Make a note of the strength and how the behavior caused you to think of the strength or strengths you have in mind.

- **Appreciate**—Tell the person what you saw, what strength you think that is, and why it matters. You can do it in an email, text, phone call, collaboration message, or in person.

Maybe you know some strengths words from a strengths assessment; there are many of them.[8] But a special language is not needed. If you don't have a name for the strength, just describe what you see. For example, my appreciation of beauty and excellence shows up by me noticing small details, admiring things in nature that others don't see, and appreciating the skill in things that others don't notice. Appreciation is shorthand for that tendency, but you can call it what you want; it is the behavior that is noteworthy.

Here is a short story for you to consider. As you read the story, underline or highlight parts that make you think of a strength.

Isla is a project manager at a large financial firm. She has been at the organization for three years. Generally, she is quiet and thoughtful. She is known for being soft-spoken and not wasting words. She does not often speak out in meetings. She likes to work with people in the background, negotiating before and after meetings with the people who appear to be the powerbrokers.

On this day, there is a meeting to discuss delays on one of the company's enterprise programs. There are about 20 people in the room, including the program sponsor, who is also the CEO of the organization.

Jamila is the project manager for one part of the overall program. Her team's work is currently on schedule but is likely to slip if the work of some of the other teams cannot be brought back on schedule. There is a lot of integration work to be completed between the teams.

The meeting starts with the CEO explaining what has been reported to him. He emphasizes that major delays are unacceptable and asks what needs to happen for the program to get back on track. Everyone, including Isla, sits quietly, many of them staring at their knees.

Tentatively, one of the project managers, Jamila, raises a hand. She is an experienced project manager. The CEO seems to look right past her as he asks one of the other people in the room for his ideas and analysis. As Tom explains that there is more work than the teams can get done in the time, Jamila again raises her hand. This time the CEO looks directly at her and asks for her ideas. She explains that the way work has been assigned to the different teams has created bottlenecks. There is a lot more overlap between the skills of the different teams than most people

---

[8] Gallup CliftonStrengths, "The 34 CliftonStrengths Themes Explain Your Talent DNA," www.gallup.com/cliftonstrengths/en/253715/34-cliftonstrengths-themes.aspx; VIA Institute on Character, "The 24 Character Strengths," www.viacharacter.org/character-strengths

realize, and if the work could be reassigned—for example, giving additional tasks to Isla's team—the program could catch up. Jamila offers to share a plan she has drawn up, but the CEO moves on and asks for other input.

Isla has a lot of respect for Jamila and believes that she has a good point—even if that will mean that Isla's team will be asked to take on more work. As the CEO returns to Tom for his suggestions, which include hiring consultants and ramping up staffing, Isla speaks up.

"I have been on this program for three years. And I have seen the work that Jamila and her team have produced, and I think she has a great point, and we should look at her plan. Even if it is not the plan we ultimately adopt, I expect it will trigger some other ideas—ideas that may mean we can avoid spending extra money to get this done. I believe, for example, that my team could carry some more of the workload to help get things back on track."

The CEO is surprised. Isla so rarely speaks up, and when she does, she is not usually so assertive. He thanks Isla for her input and invites Jamila to present her idea.

Imagine you are Jamila. What strengths feedback will you give Isla?

Now imagine you are the CEO. What strengths feedback will you give Isla?

What strengths did you see?

What behavior made you think of those strengths?

What do you appreciate about the expression of that strength?

## There Is No Right Answer: What the Coach Sees

Maybe you are wondering what I would answer to those questions. I am happy to share, but before I do, I want to stress that there is no right answer here. The beauty of strengths work is that if you think you saw it, you probably did. Strengths are positive; there is no downside to any of them. And anytime we point out a strength to a friend or colleague, we are helping to appreciate what tools are in their toolbox (tools that may have been hidden previously).

In this story, Isla is thoughtful and humble. Her usual behavior is to sit back and listen. She only speaks up when she feels she has something valuable to say. She is also brave; it is usually hard to push back on senior members of the organization. I suspect that she has a strong sense of fairness and teamwork, believing that there is value in hearing from everyone who has an idea. She is creative, knowing that the first idea may not be the winner and that just exploring ideas is likely to bring up others.

She is modeling behavior for others, encouraging them through her actions to speak up and not sit back feeling frustrated or resentful. As Isla likes to work with people in the background, she is likely to have done some homework and has possibly spoken to Jamila even before the meeting, so she is prepared. She looks out for other people and can stand up to senior management politely but firmly.

## Bringing It Back to Motivation

We started this chapter talking about motivation. So why all this discussion about strengths?

It turns out that our strengths have a lot to do with our motivation and engagement in what we do. As mentioned earlier in the chapter, people who know, show, and are encouraged to grow their character strengths feel more engaged at work. They are motivated to contribute more to a team or organizational goal—what Gallup refers to as *discretionary effort*.

People who are engaging their character strengths are more focused, more productive, more innovative, and more satisfied.

One area that has garnered quite a bit of attention is job crafting. This is when we as individuals adjust the way we do our job to consider our values, strengths, and preferences. We don't necessarily have to find a new job to feel a better fit; we can change the way we approach the jobs we have. The same is true in the rest of our life. Parenting, learning, exercising, and recuperating can all be made better by focusing on optimum use of our strengths. We don't need to use all our strengths in everything we do, but we need to engage our strengths enough to have a sense of satisfaction.

For example, recuperation for me often comes from walking outside in nature, engaging my strength of appreciation of beauty and excellence. Or enjoying a performance—a movie, music, theater, dance—where I can use my appreciation strength. If I am having a bad day, just making a conscious effort to identify one or two things to appreciate can lift my mood.

Curiosity has helped me develop healthier sleeping, eating, and exercise habits. By being curious, I created an experiment where I was the experimenter and the experiment. And I learned so much (see Chapter 8, "Being Curious: *Exploration*," for more about this story).

I can use appreciation and curiosity together to help me prioritize where it makes sense to use my curiosity and where it makes sense to dial it back—using self-regulation and even fairness.

Here are three motivational equations that work for me. What strengths will you bring together to get motivated?

**Appreciation + Curiosity + Self-Regulation + Hope + Gratitude**
**= Motivation to Prioritize and Stick to My Priorities**

**Curiosity + Deep Listening + Social Intelligence + Patience**
**+ Discernment + Love + Kindness + Honesty + Humor**
**= Motivation to Coach**

**Curiosity + Social Intelligence + Feedback of Others**
**+ Self-Regulation + Humility + Hope**
**= Motivation to Collaborate with Others**

CHAPTER

# 7

# Being Brave: *Conversation*

---

**It takes a lot of courage to show your dreams to someone else.**

—*Erma Bombeck*

---

The first time I saw that quote, I thought of my coaching clients because to me they are, by definition, brave.

As a coach, I am known for being challenging, for asking questions that turn the tables. I have been described as "not for the faint of heart" and "ruthless in my discovery," and my questions as "pointed," "probing," and "challenging." I am the same as a speaker. If you come to one of my presentations or workshops, you can expect to work—because I want to hear your ideas as much as share mine! We learn more together. We learn more by challenging assumptions and considering new perspectives.

Every client who comes to work with me is brave. Whether they are sharing their dreams, concerns, or fears, or are navigating a difficult life change. Whether they are celebrating a win or regrouping after a setback, they are sharing thoughts, feelings, and ideas that are deeply personal—and meaningful—to them.

So, what exactly do I mean when I say they are brave?

# Being Comfortable with Being Uncomfortable

My father helped me prepare for my first talk to a large audience. He was the consummate public speaker, and I was in awe of his ability to hold a conversation with a crowd, to remember the details of a complicated joke, and to get up on stage without tripping, spilling a drink, or in some other way making a fool of himself. I was convinced that he felt no fear when speaking.

I was wrong.

While working on my presentation, I lost my temper and complained that he didn't understand what I was going through.

How could he, someone who could stand up anywhere, anytime, and seemingly speak about just about any topic?

When he told me that speaking terrified him, I thought he was lying. I demanded to know how he could be anxious and do it anyway.

"I have had to get comfortable with being uncomfortable," he replied. Sometimes that's just how it is. If you are taking what you are doing seriously, it is natural to feel anxious.

But that does not have to stop you.

## Doubt and Bravery

When I first saw the results of my VIA Character Strengths assessment[1], I thought it was broken. I was taking a course about character strengths, and I was eager to take the questionnaire—I love personality assessments.

---

[1] www.viacharacter.org/surveys/takesurvey. Shown here is the first page of the free VIA Character Strengths assessment. For those who want to dive deeper into their profile independently, there are more personalized in-depth reports for purchase. In addition, the VIA Institute on Character offers a combined report exploring the combination of character strengths and the five facets of mindfulness. This combination offers a particularly insightful look at how to make the most of these positive parts of your personality.

Most of the results were unsurprising. Four of my top five strengths were appreciation of beauty and excellence, curiosity, fairness, and gratitude.

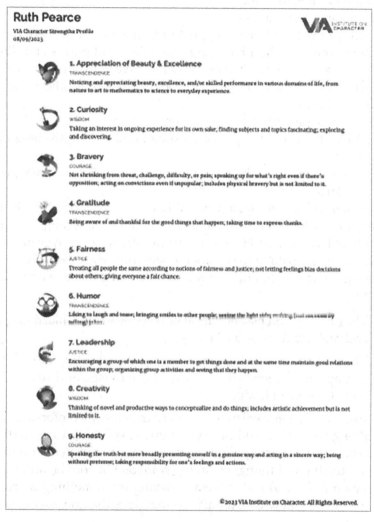

**Ruth Pearce**
VIA Character Strengths Profile
05/09/2023

**1. Appreciation of Beauty & Excellence**
TRANSCENDENCE
Noticing and appreciating beauty, excellence, and/or skilled performance in various domains of life, from nature to art to mathematics to science to everyday experience.

**2. Curiosity**
WISDOM
Taking an interest in ongoing experience for its own sake; finding subjects and topics fascinating; exploring and discovering.

**3. Bravery**
COURAGE
Not shrinking from threat, challenge, difficulty, or pain; speaking up for what's right even if there's opposition; acting on convictions even if unpopular; includes physical bravery but is not limited to it.

**4. Gratitude**
TRANSCENDENCE
Being aware of and thankful for the good things that happen; taking time to express thanks.

**5. Fairness**
JUSTICE
Treating all people the same according to notions of fairness and justice; not letting feelings bias decisions about others; giving everyone a fair chance.

**6. Humor**
TRANSCENDENCE
Liking to laugh and tease; bringing smiles to other people; seeing the light side; making (not necessarily by telling) jokes.

**7. Leadership**
JUSTICE
Encouraging a group of which one is a member to get things done and at the same time maintain good relations within the group; organizing group activities and seeing that they happen.

**8. Creativity**
WISDOM
Thinking of novel and productive ways to conceptualize and do things; includes artistic achievement but is not limited to it.

**9. Honesty**
COURAGE
Speaking the truth but more broadly presenting oneself in a genuine way and acting in a sincere way; being without pretense; taking responsibility for one's feelings and actions.

But my third ranked strength was bravery.

I stared.

Me? Brave?

No. That made no sense.

In my mind's eye, I pictured "heroes" and "heroines," people who ran into burning buildings or climbed down rock faces to rescue animals, children, and injured adults. They were people who did things for the first time where the outcome was uncertain. I pictured people willing to die or be imprisoned for their cause. Activists, firefighters, astronauts, and soldiers came to mind.

I am none of those things.

In fact, all my life I have struggled to manage anxiety. Since the age of about seven or eight, I have had a phobia about germs and illness. And I can point to times when my anxieties have gotten in the way, held me back, and led me to avoid places and events that others embrace without hesitation.

No, that assessment was wrong. I am not brave.

The VIA Character Strengths assessment ranks strengths based on a scale of 1–5.

Bravery was not just a high strength; it scored a 5. Full marks, indubitably a top strength.

I decided to keep an open mind. What was I missing? It took some bravery to consider that my own assumptions were wrong, and some curiosity to look further. Huh! There it was. Bravery—maybe just a teaspoon, but being willing to consider a new truth was, well, brave.

During my research, I discovered that there are three main kinds of bravery:

1. The physical and psychological bravery of action—like firefighters and rock climbers and astronauts.

2. The bravery involved in speaking up, representing the minority or unpopular view—like dissidents, activists, and some of our most influential leaders.

3. And, finally, personal bravery—such as being uncomfortable about doing something and doing it anyway; speaking to an audience when you have stage fright; getting on a plane even though you are terrified of flying; engaging someone in conversation when you are shy and feel awkward; asking for something when you are afraid you will be rebuffed—that date, that job, that raise.

This last explanation of bravery gave me pause. Anxiety has been a constant companion of mine, and sometimes I have given into it. But many times I felt anxious about doing something and did it anyway.

## What the Research Tells Us

Digging further into the topic, I came across the research of Dr. Cynthia Pury, who identified three components that make an act brave.[2]

---

[2] Dr. Cynthia L. S. Pury's Lab. https://purylab.wordpress.com

First, we need a *noble goal*. The goal must be something that others would recognize as having value. In addition to our personal belief that the goal is worthwhile, external recognition plays a part. For example, firefighters using their skills to rescue a person or an animal may be considered noble, but taking the same risk to recover possessions may seem inappropriate.

Second, there must be some level of *risk and fear*. Without a sense of risk and some level of anxiety, we are less engaging bravery and more engaging skill. Or maybe we are just oblivious. Firefighters are trained to use their skill and experience to make a risk assessment and determine whether the personal risk is outweighed by the potential benefit. As skilled as they are, firefighters face many situations where there is risk and apprehension as they enter a burning building or search for survivors.

Third, we have a *choice* in the matter. It is rare to be in a situation where there is no choice but to deal with the risk and fear and act. Even though firefighters have a job to do, they are generally permitted to assess a situation as too dangerous and elect to manage and limit a fire rather than go inside a burning building. Nevertheless, they often choose to go in.

---

**Although being brave is not easy, it only requires a single decisive step to embody it. The progress I have made in my journey can be attributed to taking that pivotal step.**

—*Julianne Wolfe*

---

Professor Pury's bonus insight is that we can *learn* to be braver. We can learn to manage and even reduce our fear, and to boost our inclination to choose action. And the more noble we feel our cause is, the easier it is to do.

Research also tells us that bravery, like most things, is a balancing act. For example, there is support for the idea that magical thinking can help us to accept greater challenges. A singer might brush her teeth before every performance; a teacher might have a lucky pair of socks; a tennis player might bounce the ball 14 times before serving. Maybe you have a talisman or lucky charm, a ritual or habit that makes you feel more powerful and confident.

And that is the key—this is *your* magic. We want to identify habits and practices that help us to be braver.

In contrast, however, as I discovered during my anxiety management program, magical thinking can make us *less* brave and *more* anxious. For example, have you ever thought that something you did tempted fate? That a bad outcome is inevitable because you chose to do—or not do—something?

A belief in personal magic can be a big boost when we want to take a brave action, but if we believe that magic happens *to* us, that it comes from the outside, we might become more anxious and hesitant to act.

## Getting Specific

A few years ago, I was invited to travel to India on a business trip. I was both filled with excitement and overwhelmed with anxiety.

Visiting India had long been a dream of mine. The food, the history, the culture, the people—everything about India had always intrigued me.

This was the first time I noticed that the "symptoms" of fear and excitement were very similar. My heart raced, my breathing rate increased, I had a slightly fluttery sensation in my stomach, and my head filled with images of what might happen.

I noticed that my fear was a general fear, a sense that I would not cope well with the trip. The voice in my head kept telling me that the trip was not something I could do. Between the flying, the unfamiliar location, and the heat, my inner voice told me this was not a trip I was designed to make.

In contrast, my excitement was specific. I imagined seeing new things, sampling real Indian food, meeting colleagues, laughing, exploring, and more. I imagined meeting people in person who I had only spoken to on the phone or online. I thought about the fun games I had lined up. My husband even created a cricket quiz, which entertained not just my own team but members of other teams who joined in.

But there was that dread, that general sense that this was not something I could cope with. Then, my sister, a psychologist and educator, asked me to write down all the worst things that could happen.

This was my list:

1. The plane will crash.

2. I will get sick or die. (A colleague had told me about having to be airlifted out of India when he became very ill.)

3. I will panic and embarrass myself in front of colleagues.

4. I will become claustrophobic or panic on the plane, and "lose it."

5. I will love India and not want to come back home.

6. My team members will not like me when they meet me in person.

7. I will lose my ID and all my money and not be able to get home.

8. I will have an accident and not know who I am.

9. I will faint in the heat.

10. I will get lost and no one will be able to find me.

This is just part of my list, but you get the general idea. I sent it to my sister.

She pointed out the following: One of my "fears" was that I would love it so much that I would not want to come back home! Our fears often come from places we don't expect.

Many of my fears were about what others would think of me. Most of us don't want to "lose face" or be judged as weak or cowardly. Once I realized this, I was able to work on accepting that even in the worst case, all I would lose would be my pride!

---

**While acknowledging the significance of others' perceptions of me, it is evident that we often tend to magnify their impact.**

*—Ozge Ayen Caner*

---

Some of my fears were, by anyone's standard, so unlikely as not to be relevant to the choice of whether to go. Most of those fears were easy to refute or simple to guard against. I made plans for keeping my ID and money safe. I made sure I had an international plan on my phone. I bought travel insurance. I went to my doctor for medication to help me relax on the plane.

I started to research Chennai in more detail. I consulted with the two colleagues who were traveling with me and asked for their top tips. Surprisingly, each of them said to bring an empty suitcase to bring stuff home in.

I arranged to meet my sister during my layover in London.

I even took a course in managing anxiety.

The more I got to know about where I was going, what to expect, and the most likely sources of and strategies for managing (though *not* eliminating) anxiety, the more my confidence grew.

It was not confidence that everything would go all right; it was confidence that I would *cope* with whatever happened.

In his book *The Courage Quotient*, Dr. Robert Biswas-Diener discusses two types of strategies for increasing bravery.[3] The first strategy is to control fear. Methods include using magical thinking, substituting feelings of fear with anger, researching the realities of the situation, and making contingencies.

The other strategy is to increase our willingness to act. Methods include telling others what we plan to do so that we feel accountable, engaging a defiant mindset (e.g., I will show them; I won't let this happen), protecting or collaborating with others, and being willing to fail.

In my work as a coach, I have found that bravery increases when we learn to *tolerate* discomfort, focusing on the belief that we can handle it, that we can cope with the good and the bad.

Trying to *control* fear is often a losing battle—one I have lost several times myself. But when we accept fear as natural, as appropriate, and as providing useful information, then we can choose what to do with it. We have a full spectrum of choice, from avoiding the situation to preparing as much as possible for it, to embracing it!

## Changing the Narrative with Coaching

### Reframe #1: I Will Cope

What would you do if you were 5 percent braver?

Early in my coaching practice, a client who had not left his home in more than 2 years contacted me. We worked together for some time, exploring options for making small changes. One day I asked him to think about what he would if he were 5 percent braver.

He called in to the next coaching session and said, "I want to make a plan for going down to the mailbox and collecting my mail!" He had not done this in more than 2 years.

In Chapter 5, "Being Hopeful: Expectation," when I discussed hope, I considered the power of visualization. Visualization also has benefits when we are trying to increase our bravery.

**Coaching question 1: What do you visualize when you think about going to the mailbox?**

---

[3] Robert Biswas-Diener, *The Courage Quotient: How Science Can Make You Braver*, San Francisco: Jossey-Bass, 2012, 23.

The client pondered and answered, "I open my front door, step out, walk down the hallway, get in the elevator, go to the front desk, unlock my mailbox, and take out the mail. Then I come back."

The entire description of a journey that would take about 10–15 minutes took less than 30 seconds to recount.

"Let's go through that again in more detail," I suggested.

**Coaching question 2: Before opening your front door, what will you do to get ready?**

He replied:

1. I will choose what I am going to wear.

2. I will brush my hair and teeth.

3. I will put on outdoor shoes.

4. I will pick up a bag to bring the mail back in.

**Coaching question 3: Now, what happens when you open the front door to your apartment? What will you see? Smell? Hear? Feel? Taste?**

The client continued, "Well, when I first open the door, I will see my neighbor's door. They work during the day, so I probably won't bump into them. But I know they often use a slow cooker for meals, so I might be able to smell some food. And the last time I looked out, they had scratches on the door paint as though their dog had been scratching. I wonder if that has been repainted yet.

"I got a notice from the landlord that the communal areas were being recarpeted, so I expect the hallway will look different. I hope they installed something a little nicer than the brown carpet that was there before."

The client continued, reflecting on how each of his senses would be activated. He talked about what he would smell, what he would hear, and what he would see as he took the journey to the front desk. He talked about the smell of food and cleaning supplies, the feel of the carpet under his shoes, and the sensation of the elevator descending. He planned to chew gum to ensure that his mouth tasted fresh and minty. He planned to say hello to the doorperson, who had for so long brought his groceries to his door. He anticipated the doorperson's surprise at seeing him downstairs and smiled.

He considered strategies for managing any anxiety he might feel and decided that he would count to 10 before deciding whether to continue. He also decided to set incremental goals so that he could check off each landmark and measure his progress. And he carried in his pocket a small elephant a close friend had given him to remind him to be strong and tolerate any discomfort. He also decided to tell his friend of his plan, to have someone other than his coach keep him accountable.

He chose a mantra: "I will cope with whatever happens!"

The next day, he texted me that he had made it down to pick up his mail. He had a conversation with the doorperson, who was indeed surprised and pleased to see him, and he even stepped outside the front door to help someone struggling with their shopping bags.

He was tired—bravery is often tiring—but excited to have accomplished his goal. He told me, "It was even better than I imagined. And I have much more confidence that I will cope—even if things don't go as planned."

Just as visualization can help us to develop greater hope, it can help us to be braver. And, as discussed previously, bravery can be developed incrementally. One percent braver a day for 70 days is 100% braver at the end!

---

**15 QUESTIONS TO CULTIVATE YOUR BRAVERY**

1. What will change for you after you've achieved your goal?
2. On a scale of 1–10, what is your risk/fear level for achieving your goal?
3. How will you reduce your fear level by 1?
4. What will you feel like after accomplishing your goal?
5. Where will you feel that in your body?
6. When have you felt that way previously?
7. What can you learn from that experience?
8. What will you see?
9. What will you hear?
10. What will you smell?
11. What will you taste?
12. What will you feel and where in your body will you feel it?
13. What preparation do you need?
14. When will you move forward on your journey to your goal?
15. Who will you tell about your plan?

---

## Reframe #2: Feeling Bad Is Good

When exploring bravery with clients, I am often struck by how many see fear as a weakness. They assume others don't worry as much as they do, that others are more confident and have higher self-esteem. They often assume that their fear means they are not up to their goal.

Fear tells us something. Often, it is telling us something helpful.

For example, when I am high up, I feel anxious about falling—or jumping. This "fear" reminds me to pay attention to where I place my feet and what I hold on to. It also encourages me to consider realistically how good I am at balancing, the wind, and so on.

Fear of public speaking reminds us to be prepared. It is feeling a sense of responsibility for the audience and generally is helping us to make good choices that make our speech more likely to be successful.

Anxiety before an exam reminds us to study and stay focused.

Fear is "bad" only when it so overwhelming and debilitating that we cannot function effectively because of it.

Questions I have heard used in coaching include the following:

1. On a scale of 1–10, what is a reasonable level of fear in this situation?
2. What is your level of fear?
3. What would it take to reduce that level by 1?
4. What will happen if you don't see this through?
5. What will happen if you do see it through?
6. How will you feel when the situation is over?

## Reframe #3: Bravery Can Be Developed a Little at a Time

As mentioned several times in this book, making incremental changes is a path to lasting and significant improvement. Two percent improvement a day for 35 days = 100% improvement. And bravery is something that can be increased incrementally too. Many clients find that tracking their progress is helpful. Some use a journal; others, their phone. One of the biggest challenges we face is effectively recognizing and celebrating our small wins. We are much more likely to sustain change and growth when we stop to take stock of small accomplishments. Change is not achieved by consistency of outcomes; it is achieved by consistency of effort. When we record and celebrate that effort, we find it easier to maintain.

Have you ever reached the end of a year and looked back and wondered how you got to where you are? How often do you look back and realize that you achieved goals you did not dream about or that seemed out of reach? That is because we change incrementally and cannot always appreciate the change until the end!

# Case Study: Jamal

Jamal has been afraid of going to the dentist since he was 7 years old. As a child, he had two teeth removed during a regular checkup. He felt unprepared and blindsided. One of the family stories about him was that he jumped out of the dentist's chair, ran away from the nurse, and had to be held in the chair by his mother.

Just before going to college, Jamal experienced a toothache and realized it had been more than 10 years since his last dentist visit. His parents gave up trying to persuade him to go to the dentist. He was an adult now, so the decision was up to him.

He decided to explore how to overcome his fear with his coach.

While someone going to the dentist might not fit with Cynthia Pury's original concept of a "noble cause," I know plenty of people who would argue that overcoming the fear of the dentist's office is worthwhile. It is, of course, a choice whether to go—although a worsening toothache can make it feel less so! And it is reasonable to be trepidatious about going to the dentist. After all, it's not very comfortable to have someone else's hands in your mouth, and even with pain medication, treatment is usually uncomfortable.

When asked about a reasonable level of fear, Jamal thought for a moment and answered: "Five." His coach asked him to expand on his answer, and Jamal explained that being at the dentist is unpredictable, you cannot be sure what they will recommend, and sometimes the pain continues after the appointment. At the same time, it is unlikely to be dangerous or life-threatening, and the discomfort will not last forever.

When asked what *his* level of fear is, he immediately answered, *"Ten!"* Then he laughed nervously and said, "OK, eight."

"That is a bit of a gap," the coach observed. "What do you need in order to reduce your level of fear to a seven?"

Jamal thought for a bit and answered:

1. I want to find a dentist who specializes in treating nervous patients.

2. I would like to visit the dentist's office and meet the staff, to make sure they are going to be supportive.

3. I would need to meet the dentist beforehand and explain my concerns and see what the options are.

4. Maybe I could just sit in the waiting room a couple of times to get used to the smell and the sounds. It has been a while since I have been there!

"What happens if you don't go to the dentist?" the coach asked.

"Well, I suspect this toothache will get worse, and maybe, instead of a filling, I will end up having the tooth removed. I might have other things that need to get treated that I don't even know about. In the end, I could lose or damage my teeth, and I don't want false teeth at the age of 30!"

"What will happen if you see this through?" the coach replied.

"My toothache will go away, and I will know what needs to be done to look after my teeth. I hope I will have more confidence for the future and will have a dentist I can work with going forward. My mother will throw a party," Jamal joked.

"And how will you feel when it is done?" asked the coach.

"I will feel relieved. I will feel proud. I will also feel more like an adult and less silly—I don't even like to tell friends how long it's been since I went to the dentist. I think I will feel taller, and I will definitely have more confidence for the future of my dental care. As I think about it, I suspect that just one OK experience would make a huge difference."

Jamal researched his options and went to visit a dental office. He immediately liked the people behind the counter, and when he explained his anxiety, they were sympathetic and even told him the dentist could provide something to help him relax. As Jamal left, the nurse asked him how he was, and he answered, "This is my favorite dental office ever!" He noted that his anxiety level going back was about a seven.

Two days later, Jamal went back to sit in the waiting room. He didn't have an appointment and initially was self-conscious, but then started talking to a little girl waiting for her first extraction. Before he knew it, Jamal was assuring the girl that it would be OK. "It won't hurt for long, and you're tough enough to handle it," he reassured her.

Jamal turned to the receptionist and proclaimed, "I am at the dentist! My favorite thing!" At the time he was joking, but later, as he left the office, he realized it was not such an exaggeration. He was already feeling better about the visit. He still had anxiety, but it was now a 5 out of 10 instead of an 8. With his anxiety at a reasonable level, he was able to stop berating himself.

Jamal changed his attitude incrementally. He started by exploring the specifics of his fear with his coach, and then he did his homework to find a dentist that increased his sense of safety and confidence. He also added a new piece to the puzzle: humor.

And, finally, he focused on someone else, which can be an effective strategy to enhance our bravery.

---

**Bravery is doing something even though you are scared. I find it easier to be brave when it comes to standing up for others, so I often ask myself, "what would I advise someone else to do in the face of this difficulty?"**

*—Jana Wardian, making meaning by being Nana and striving to reduce the stress of being a patient*

---

## Reframe #4: Bravery Is Sometimes Knowing When to Say No

This chapter has focused on ways to make ourselves say yes, accept more challenges, tolerate discomfort, and embrace change.

There are times, however, when saying no is the bravest action we can take. How many people do you know who think "no" is the hardest word to say?

Maybe the inability to say no stems from the fear of missing out (FOMO). We are afraid of what others will think of us, or we overestimate our capacity for getting things done. We forget that we have finite amounts of time and energy.

The result is often that we overcommit ourselves and end up doing things less well than we would like. Rather than satisfying everyone, we leave everyone less than content.

There are several ways we can make the word "no" easier to tolerate for ourselves—and others.

For example, we can use a set of criteria to help us decide whether an invitation, request, or opportunity fits with our priorities. Creating the criteria ahead of time makes it much easier to rationally consider our options. We can always decide to ignore our usual criteria and take a different route, but that becomes a decision, not the default response.

Dr. Todd Kashdan, author of *The Art of Insubordination* and creator of the Provoked Newsletter, uses the following criteria to determine whether to accept a request:[4]

- *Autonomy*: Will I be given sufficient freedom to think, act, and develop ideas?

- *Creativity*: How novel/unique/original is this opportunity?

---

[4] Todd Kashdan, "Decisions with Purpose," *Provoked* (blog), July 20, 2023, https://toddkashdan.substack.com/p/decisions-with-purpose

- *Impact*: If everything works as planned, how will others benefit?

- *Money*: Will I receive fair compensation for putting in the extra effort alongside my main job, family, friends, while also dedicating significant time and energy?

- *Friends*: Will I be able to spend more time with the people I enjoy being around the most?

If the opportunity does not meet a satisfactory number of these criteria, Dr. Kashdan declines. The process of considering these criteria prompts him to fully consider his choices—and their potential consequences.

One of the things I find most difficult in my coaching practice is saying no. Whether it involves a coaching opportunity, a speaking engagement, or a writing option, I want to say *"yes!"* to all of them. So, I too have had to develop a set of criteria I can use to prioritize.

My considerations include the following:

1. How excited am I now to agree to the engagement?
2. How excited will I be when the time comes (especially when the engagement involves travel)? And how I will feel in 6 months if I don't say yes?
3. Who is the audience and how will they benefit?
4. Do I have any other commitments?
5. What will I need to decline in order to accept this opportunity?
6. How does the opportunity align with or advance my biggest goals?

I use a points-based ranking system and rarely say yes to anything that doesn't score at least 30 out of 50.

These criteria have helped me to no end. Defining my criteria *before* I have to make a decision makes it easier to be dispassionate and mindful about my choices, however tempted I may initially be to say yes.

Saying no when we want to please people is another way of being brave. We may be uncomfortable saying no, but we will be even more uncomfortable if we overcommit and have to back out or change plans later. And there are ways to say no that still feel constructive. If we want to protect or build a relationship, then we may want to say no to the original request and offer something smaller and more manageable. For example, when asked to present at a conference and the timing is not convenient, I can say, "No, but I can suggest some other great speakers you could consider," or I can offer to record a session ahead of time.

## Fired Up with Curiosity

I have long believed that we are not just what we start with. We are more than our upbringing, formal education, habits, and beliefs. We can learn, grow, and change.

Over the years, I have found that starting with hope, strengths, and bravery can take us a long way. Chapter 5 considered ways to increase your capacity for hope, Chapter 6, "Being Strong: Motivation," explored building on your strengths, and this chapter discussed being brave. Chapter 8, "Being Curious: Exploration," builds on these components by discussing curiosity—both from the coach's and the client's perspective.

### QUESTIONS TO ASK TO INCREASE YOUR BRAVERY

Here are some questions to consider as you work to increase your bravery:

- What is a conversation that you want or need to have with someone else? What will you do to make yourself a little braver?
- If you were 5 percent braver, what would you do differently? What would you say?
- How will you feel once you've taken the brave step?
- What is one thing you can do to reduce your fear or anxiety?
- What is one thing you can do to make it more likely that you will act?
- How does the choice you make between saying yes and no serve your purpose or goals?
- What are your criteria for saying yes or no?
- What would your superhero/heroine do?
- How will you be 2 percent braver tomorrow?

CHAPTER

# 8

# Being Curious: *Exploration*

Research is formalized curiosity. It is poking and prying with a purpose.

—*Zora Neale Hurston*

Check out a coach training website, and most likely you will find a reference to curiosity as a core coaching virtue. It is generally accepted wisdom that a coach who lacks curiosity is likely to be ineffective.

Of course, we want coaches to be trustworthy, empathetic, compassionate, on the side of our client, focused, etc. And at the end of the day, we want coaches to be just curious enough to help their clients achieve great outcomes. A coach without curiosity is like a pitcher without a ball—or something to that effect, anyway!

When I began this chapter, I expected it to be one of the shorter chapters. However, as I reviewed the research and writings on curiosity, I realized that, although obvious, it is not a simple topic. We cannot just "be curious" as coaches and clients. Curiosity is most effective when it is focused, intentional, thoughtful, and managed. Not every question is created equal; they don't all deserve to be asked—or answered.

# What Is Curiosity?

Most people are quick to notice that I am curious—I am sure some might even say nosy! There are few things that don't hold my interest. I can even get curious about why the patterns of holes are as they are on acoustic tiles in hospital waiting rooms. I attribute my curiosity to my father, who was incurably curious. And yet there is, I believe, a significant difference. I can turn it off or at least dial it down.

When I was a child (way before the Internet and smartphones), practically every meal was interrupted by my father having to look something up. If he heard a fact that he found doubtful, or one of us asked a question that he couldn't answer, he would jump up, rush into the living room, and go hunting for the right book to look up the details.

We had endless reference books, for which I am grateful, including books of famous quotations, encyclopedias, atlases, and foreign language dictionaries. It was a wonderful environment to grow up in and one that was very different from my parents' childhood experiences, but—and it is a big but—my father had zero tolerance for the discomfort of not knowing. He could not wait until the meal was over to answer a question. And if he did not have the right book at the house, he would drive to the library or call someone he knew would have the answer.

I had always assumed that curiosity was just that urge to know—a tendency for us all to ask, "But why?" I believed it was reactive—that something catches our eye and enters our consciousness, and curiosity is triggered.

I also thought curiosity could be exhausting. In school, I saw children told by beleaguered teachers to "ask fewer questions." And we have all seen the parent who, exhausted by the endless flow of questions, finally says, "Because I say so!" We don't want to do it, but sometimes we just cannot help ourselves. The intensity and durability of the other person's curiosity wear us down. Dad was like that because he would not—or could not—stop. And one of the most frustrating aspects of his curiosity was when we would ask a question and he would answer something entirely different. When challenged, he would say, "I am answering the question you should have asked!"

In 2016, I stumbled across a book called *Curious* by Dr. Todd Kashdan.[1] Published in 2010, *Curious* examines not only the benefits of curiosity but also the components of it.

---

[1] Todd Kashdan, *Curious?: Discover the Missing Ingredient to a Fulfilling Life* (New York: Harper Perennial, 2010).

According to Kashdan, curiosity comprises the following:

- *Intensity* refers to the strength of our feeling of curiosity, our urge to know and to experience new things.
  One of my father's qualities that I most admired was his openness to new ideas. He was an iconoclast in many ways. It could also be his most annoying quality.

- *Frequency* refers to how often our curiosity is stirred up.
  Some people seem to be attracted—or distracted—by every shiny new thing. Others are rarely consumed with curiosity, but when they are, they feel it deeply. And still others just seem to take things at face value and rarely feel compelled to pull back the curtain or go a level deeper.

- *Durability* refers to how long the curiosity persists.
  Continuing with the example of my father, he could hunt down an answer—to a question or a crossword clue or an address—for hours and days. He would keep going until he was satisfied that he had the answer or there was no answer.

- *Breadth* refers to the range of things that people are curious about.
  I can safely say that there was not much that did not pique my father's interest. And I am the same. To me, everything seems to have the possibility of value, a connection to things I already know or think I know. Every new experience could enhance my skills as a coach and a person. Whatever happens, I am curious to learn what I can learn about me, other people, and the environment.

- *Depth* refers to how far we go with our interest.
  Do we turn our interest into a lifetime of learning, or do we scratch the initial itch and move on? My father would often provide updates days or weeks later on a topic that we had all long since forgotten. His curiosity about language seemed to be bottomless!

On reading these ideas, I became curious (!) about the interplay between my father and the people around him. How did his curiosity influence others? How did their curiosity (or sometimes lack of it) impact him? Nothing seemed to make him sadder or more tired than having a conversation with someone who had no interest in finding out more or looking beyond the obvious. I have no doubt that your capacity for curiosity would be the number one measure of your value for my dad!

As I considered the withering looks my mother would cast as he leapt up from the table, and the "Oh, Dad!" comments that my sister and

I would make, I constructed the following chart using the five measures described in Kashdan's book.

A score of 1 means that this attribute is not significant for the person, while a score of 5 means it is core. This table gives examples.

| PERSON | INTENSITY | FREQUENCY | DURABILITY | BREADTH | DEPTH |
|--------|-----------|-----------|------------|---------|-------|
| Father | 5 | 5 | 5 | 5 | 5 |
| Self | 4 | 4 | 4 | 5 | 3 |
| Mother | 2 | 3 | 3 | 2 | 3 |
| Sister | 4 | 4 | 5 | 3 | 5 |

These are my best guesses, of course.

Is one of the reasons why my mother spent a lot of time alone in her room seeking some "peace and quiet" because our curiosity was exhausting? She used to say that life was full of enough uncertainty, and she didn't need to be curious about things that didn't directly concern her. And yet she was a social worker, and by all accounts, a good one, so she could be curious enough.

## Matchmaking in Coaching and Other Helping Situations

What is your level of curiosity? How intensely do you feel curiosity? What topics interest you?

If a friend asks you for help with a personal problem, how important is it that you be at least a little curious? And how curious should you be?

Now, think about what you would want in a coach or other helper. Do you want them to be relentless with their questions? Do you want them to have a personal investment in finding the answer? Here is a chart to help you think about your answers. This table can be used to fill in for yourself.

| PERSON | INTENSITY | FREQUENCY | DURABILITY | BREADTH | DEPTH |
|--------|-----------|-----------|------------|---------|-------|
| Coach | | | | | |
| Client | | | | | |

We will come back to this question later.

## Case Study: Tegan

Tegan arrives at her coach's office clearly flustered. The coach wonders what is going on, but this is Tegan's session, so the coach will follow Tegan's lead. They have been working together for some time, and the coach trusts that if Tegan wants to talk about what is bothering her, she will.

After the usual greetings, the coach asks, "What do you want to focus on for our session today?"

Rather than explaining what is going on and why she is so flustered, Tegan quickly answers that she really does not feel ready for a coaching session. She has not had time to think about a topic, and she is harried and distracted, she explains.

The coach is curious about what is going on. Coaches are human after all, but she is not sure that getting Tegan to explain is in Tegan's own best interest.

So, rather than asking an obvious question—the question that we would ask a friend, for example—maybe "What's up?" or "What's going on?" the coach asks the following question:

"What's most helpful to you in this moment?"

Surprised, Tegan pauses, draws a breath, and answers, "I just need a moment to catch my breath." The coach sits back and waits while Tegan calms her breathing, closes her eyes, and seems to melt into the chair. After a few moments, she is ready, and they start the session. Tegan is focused and spends the time exploring options for a promotion. The coach never does find out what made Tegan so agitated.

Of course, an argument could be made for just naming the elephant in the room and asking the obvious question.

First, however, the coach must ask herself a question: "What is the purpose of the question I am about to ask?"

We use curiosity in coaching for the benefit of the client, not to satisfy our need for answers! So, the question we must always have in mind is "What is the purpose?"

I have lost count of the number of times I have been curious about a client but didn't satisfy my curiosity because it did not serve them.

And often this mindset leads to some of the most powerful and impactful questions a coach will ask. Examples include the following:

1. When a client described a situation at work and started using industry jargon, the coach asked, "What do I need to know in order to be a support to you?" rather than, "What does that mean?" The client elected to start using everyday phrases and, in so doing, recognized a communication problem with colleagues from a different area of the organization.

2. Another coach, seeking to help a client consider his interactions with the people around him at work asked, "Do you happen to know your IQ?" The client explained he did and went on to explore

how his IQ and the speed with which he processes information could be intimidating to others. That coach never knew what the IQ of the client was, only that it was high enough that many people could not keep up with his thinking—or that it was a possibility worth considering.

3.  A third coach, working with a newly promoted manager, was told, "As a manager, it is my job to ensure that everyone has exactly what they need to get the work done and that they know exactly how to do it; I make sure it gets done. My boss's job is to coach me on how to do it, but they are not doing that!" The coach asked, "What would you do differently if you knew your boss didn't know how to coach you?"

## Why Curiosity Is Powerful

There is substantial research that suggests curiosity is a good thing. We learn by being curious. Curiosity and intelligence levels seem to go hand in hand—with evidence that increased curiosity results in higher intelligence. In 2018, the *Harvard Business Review* even published a spotlight series of three articles about curiosity.[2] The first article laid out the business case for curiosity. From fewer errors in decision-making to greater innovation, curiosity can be enormously beneficial in business. Without curiosity, we would not explore or ask, "What is beyond the horizon?" We would not ask, "How can we do this differently or better?" Without curiosity, we would not have vaccines or understand how medication works. Every discovery in human history has been because someone somewhere wondered:

How?

Why?

What if?

Where?

Who?

When?

[2] Francesca Gino, "The Business Case for Curiosity," *Harvard Business Review*, July 8, 2021, https://hbr.org/2018/09/the-business-case-for-curiosity

In 2010, Dr. Kashdan and his colleagues shared their research on the five components of curiosity. Going beyond the ideas of intensity and frequency we explored previously, the research revealed there are five components that are distinct and can be measured separately. (There is even an assessment to help you measure the different types of curiosity.)[3] Here are the five components:

- *Deprivation sensitivity (or tolerance of not knowing)*—This is a measure of the drive to fill a gap in our knowledge. When we fill that gap, we feel not just pleasure and satisfaction, but relief.

- *Joyous exploration*—This is the excitement and pleasure we feel when we learn more about the world. It is the enjoyment of discovering something new, stretching our horizons, knowing something we didn't previously know. This is where, on its own, curiosity can take us by surprise. We discover something we weren't looking for and take pleasure in our good fortune. On its own, joyous exploration may not drive us to act on our curiosity.

- *Stress tolerance*—To satisfy our curiosity, we must be able to tolerate a period of greater uncertainty. We must enjoy novelty. What we previously believed or thought we knew is called into question, and while we conduct our research, we must be able to tolerate not knowing for sure. If our learning is going to be solid, we need the patience to double-check to verify our findings. We cannot jump on the first explanation that seems to make sense.

- *Social curiosity*—This is a measure of how much we seek to know about and from others. For some, there is little interest in finding out what others think or feel, in knowing more about their experiences or beliefs. For others, getting insights into other people can lead to nosiness and intrusiveness.

- *Thrill seeking*—This is a measure of the risks we are prepared to take to satisfy our curiosity. It could be the difference between wondering what skydiving is like and actually booking a jump, or investing a lot of money to find out if you can get into space.

After all those years with my dad, imagine how satisfying it was to read that one of those components is deprivation sensitivity?

---

[3] Todd B. Kashdan and Jonathan Rottenberg, "Psychological Flexibility as a Fundamental Aspect of Health," *Clinical Psychology Review*, 30, no. 7 (November 2010):865–878. https://doi.org/10.1016/j.cpr.2010.03.001

# Case Study: Jamal

When Jamal calls in to his coaching session, he sounds gloomy. He tells his coach that his girlfriend has complained that he is not very curious. "She wants me to ask more about her," he says. "And she is always wanting to ask me about my family, where I grew up, and how I made the choices I made! It's exhausting. I sometimes try to change the subject to what I am looking forward to, but she always wants to go back to the past and ask more about that."

The coach asks, "What *are* you curious about?"

Jamal thinks for a minute and responds, "I love science! I want to know about new discoveries and new inventions—everything from new species to new medications. When I was young, I considered it a lucky day when I found the science section of the newspaper left behind on the train or the bus! If I hear about something new on the news, I want to go to my computer and look it up right away. At the same time, however, I want to make sure I get things done first, that I don't fritter my time away satisfying my curiosity rather than meeting my commitments.

"I am not really interested in knowing about people's personal history or talking about mine. I think we are who we are now. I am sure our past influences who we are and how we behave, but I want to focus on the here and now and the future. I am happy to explore plans for what is coming. I get excited by thinking about what might be possible in the years to come. But what happened when I was 5 years old is not really all that relevant to me. And as for my girlfriend, she is wonderful and interesting. She is studying law, and she comes home with interesting ideas and things we can debate. That is much more interesting to me than what she was like as a girl, when I didn't even know her."

The coach asks what Jamal knows about curiosity, and when he says he does not know much, they explore the five components. Then the coach hands Jamal a chart (shown below) and invites him to score each component out of 5.

| PERSON | DEPRIVATION SENSITIVITY | JOYOUS EXPLORATION | STRESS TOLERANCE | SOCIAL CURIOSITY | THRILL SEEKING | TOTAL |
|---|---|---|---|---|---|---|
| Jamal | 2 | 4 | 3 | 2 | 2 | 13 |
| Friend | 4 | 4 | 4 | 5 | 3 | 20 |

Jamal thinks about each category and enters scores for him and his girlfriend. He takes his time, thinking carefully about each component and reviewing the explanations. After completing the grid, he nods and says, "Yeah, that seems about right. My curiosity is specific and regulated. She is generally more curious and more motivated to find things out. Maybe that is just as well because she is going to be a lawyer! I think I will show this to her so we can discuss it more objectively."

This is an example of where measurement and comparison can help clarify what is happening between two people.

# Why Curiosity Can Be Too Much

As previously mentioned, one of my top character strengths is curiosity. In general, it serves me well. At times in my life when I have felt disconnected from others and out of place, curiosity has kept me engrossed and engaged. When starting a new job or training program, curiosity has helped me to get past the early frustrations of not knowing and to trust that the knowledge will develop layer by layer. When faced with challenges for myself or friends and family, curiosity has meant I could focus on finding options, discovering what is possible and helping build a strategy instead of sinking into a pit of despair.

Then there are times when curiosity is *not* such a wonderful ally. There are two main ways that my natural intense curiosity can be detrimental.

## Curiosity as the Antithesis of Mindfulness

In the West, there has been an increasing interest—one might even say curiosity—in recent years about the power and importance of mindfulness. It can settle the mind, ease the conscience, increase focus, and soothe pain.

One of the most well-known Western experts in mindfulness is Jon Kabat-Zinn. He is the creator of the Mindfulness-Based Stress Reduction program and author of the book *Full Catastrophe Living*,[4] which was based on his work with people suffering from chronic pain.

His definition of mindfulness has been the go-to for coaches and other helping professionals. He says, "Mindfulness is awareness that

---

[4] Jon Kabat-Zinn, *Full Catastrophe Living: Using the Wisdom of Your Body and Mind to Face Stress, Pain, and Illness* (New York: Bantam Books, 2013).

arises through paying attention, on purpose, in the present moment, non-judgmentally. . .in the service of self-understanding and wisdom."[5]

In the field of character strengths, "Mindfulness is the self-regulation of attention with an attitude of curiosity, openness, and acceptance."[6] I have always liked this definition because it is simple and clear. And it has helped me understand why meditation and mindfulness have always been such a challenge for me. This two-prong definition is where I may get into trouble. Curiosity I have aplenty. Self-regulation is not even a middle strength! In fact, it is usually the bottom strength in my VIA Character Strengths assessment.

For me, and I suspect for many others, curiosity can be a *huge* distraction. The story about my father always jumping up in the middle of meals to search for answers is amusing, but it also meant that family dinners never went smoothly. My father modeled for me that paying undivided attention to something—or, more importantly, someone—is difficult and unnecessary. I became tolerant and even expected interruptions, and that meant I was an interrupter myself. (I still am in many circumstances.) Hardly the recipe for effective coaching, friendships, and team building!

Even when other people are not involved, my curiosity has led me astray. While doing homework for school, I would get distracted from the paper I was writing as I went down the rabbit hole of a single solitary— but intriguing—fact. Hours would go by, and instead of completing the homework steadily and with time to spare, I would be scrambling to finish and would go to school cranky.

Many is the night when 5 or 10 minutes of reading before going to sleep has resulted in me still being up at 3 a.m. reading under the covers with a flashlight. Just one more chapter. Just one more paragraph. Just one more fact.

I was one of those children at school who was asked not to keep putting her hand up to ask questions. One teacher spoke to my parents about it, and it was gently explained to me that all my questions might intimidate the other children who want to ask things too. It is funny, looking back, because as shy as I was, I was never shy about asking a question, challenging assumptions, or asking for a more complete explanation.

---

[5] "Jon Kabat-Zinn: Defining Mindfulness," Mindful, January 11, 2017, www.mindful.org/jon-kabat-zinn-defining-mindfulness
[6] Scott R. Bishop, et al. "Mindfulness: A Proposed Operational Definition, *Clinical Psychology: Science and Practice* 11, no. 3 (2004): 230–241.

And I was the person who, in a seminar while exploring character strengths back in 2016, realized that a month without curiosity sounded like a vacation. Hmm, a little overuse of this go-to-strength? I thought so.

I had seen people doing the character strength subtraction exercise (see the upcoming sidebar) get excited by time off from being kind to others!

Anytime we lean on a strength too much, it can become detrimental to us and to others. And curiosity, as powerful and positive as it can be, is no different.

### CURIOUS ABOUT THE CHARACTER STRENGTHS SUBTRACTION EXERCISE?

This practice, which is used in many forms of psychology and therapy, is intended to help us understand what it would be like to give up something that is core to us. In the case of character strengths, we are using the exercise to truly appreciate our top strengths—those that are an essential part of us. All too often we don't recognize that a habitual behavior we adopt reflects a strength. We might think everyone behaves that way. An example of using the subtraction exercise is available on the Greater Good Science Center—Greater Good In Action website, which you can find at https://ggia.berkeley.edu/practice/mental_subtraction_positive_events.

Follow these instructions to experience the character strengths subtraction exercise first hand

1. Look at a list of strengths. They could be the 24 VIA Character strengths or a list of strengths we have brainstormed earlier in the session.

2. Choose one to focus on that you consider to be essential to you, one that you believe others would call out in you as well.

3. Think about times when you use that strength and what it feels like to use that strength. Recollect the physical feelings, the thoughts, the emotions that you experience when you use this strength.

4. Now imagine 30 days without it.

   In groups, this is when there is usually a long pause as faces fall. Then I give examples—if you are curious, you cannot look things up, ask other people questions, Google things, read a book, watch a TED Talk, or go to a library.

   If you are kind, you cannot do something spontaneous for someone, you don't hold open the door, stoop to help someone when they have dropped something, or put an arm around a loved one who is upset.

5. Now share a word to describe how that feels.

   Some typical words I get back include the following:

| | | |
|---|---|---|
| Empty | Not me | Dishonest |
| Sad | Depressed | Devastated |
| Hollow | Hopeless | Adrift |
| Lost | Pointless | Cold |

And then occasionally there is someone who hesitantly raises a hand and says something like, "Actually, that sounds kind of nice!" It has happened often enough that I always invite people to consider that it might be somewhat appealing because they may be shy to say so when everyone else is expressing the sadness of giving up a strength.

## Curiosity as Overcompensation for Nerves

Another way my curiosity can get overplayed and be less than helpful is when I am stressed. One of my least favorite things to do is going to large social gatherings, networking events, and other places where I am unfamiliar with the people and the place. When I am stressed, look out. I am curious with abandon. More than once I have found myself pounding a fellow guest with questions about their family, their route to the event, their work, and their hobbies.

For some people, who, like me, are feeling awkward, it can take the pressure off. As long as I keep asking questions and they keep answering, we will be able to keep the conversation going.

For others, though, it feels like a version of the Spanish Inquisition. The other person feels trapped and unable to get away until they see someone they know and wave or find another excuse to slip away somewhere else. One party guest told me that they thought they were at the wrong party! I saw them later laughing and enjoying themselves with people they knew.

This use of curiosity to mask—it does not really relieve—stress is another habit that doesn't necessarily serve a coach well. And it is another habit I learned from my father.

Unknown to me, my father was uncomfortably socially awkward, and although he was often asked to speak at dinners and conferences, he found public speaking to be nerve-wracking. So, he would fall back on curiosity. There was no topic too dull and no question too trivial to keep a conversation going. He once asked a friend to our house for tea and got so distracted by the questions he had for his friend that he forgot to make the tea and his friend left without refreshment. If my father did run out of questions, which was rare, he always had a joke to tell. An empty silence was anathema to him!

## Cultivating Healthy Curiosity as a Coach

Before I could be an effective coach, I had to learn to manage—or regulate—my curiosity. At first, it was not easy. My mind would chase down rabbit holes opened by the client. I would find myself a long way removed from what the client was saying as I thought about some earlier remark.

With practice, I have been able to develop a quiet focus. As soon as I step into a coaching or speaking environment, my client or the audience become my entire focus. I can feel the rest of the world, the rest of life, moving away as though the sound of it is fading. There is a spotlight on my fellow traveler or travelers, and I am immersed in following the threads of their thinking, musings, and ideas.

As a coach, I want to ask questions that help you, not questions that merely satisfy me. And by being focused on whether my questions are meeting my self-imposed requirements, I take control of my wandering mind. I want to be interested enough in you to maintain my attention and to build rapport, but not so curious that I lose sight of the purpose of the session and start asking questions for my own pleasure or relief. As I get more coaching and training under my belt, I become less of an active participant in your process and more of a witness and guide.

I also want to ask the best sorts of questions—open questions that encourage contemplation by you, the client, non-leading questions that leave all possibilities open, and clear, concise questions that don't take so much thought that they might distract you.

And when I do ask a question, I want to be open to any answer—even the answer to a question I did not mean to ask! The client's interpretation of what the question means is often as useful as the answer they come up with.

We refer to coaching questions as *generative questions*. They are open-ended, challenge assumptions and the status quo, usually have multiple possible answers, and often lead directly to more questions.

Of course, this is not to say we never ask closed questions—for clarification or to help the client reach a decision. As coaching skill increases, we can see situations where a different kind of question might be effective. But much of coaching is about keeping options open, not shutting options down.

For coaches who are reading this, a wonderful book by Dr. Robert Biswas-Diener called *Positive Provocation* explores 25 coaching questions to advance your coaching practice.[7] The beauty of this book is that it challenges some of the beliefs and assumptions we have about the questions we ask and the things we share as coaches. It explores things like when and whether to ask *why* questions, whether to share personal experiences, whether coaching really is nondirective, and why it is hard to go from being good to great as a coach.

But truly context-sensitive coaching, where the coach provides not just want the client knows they want but also what they may not yet realize they need, takes a lifetime to develop. So, in general, sticking to coaching with open-ended, challenging but supportive questions, as free as humanly possible from bias and prejudgment, leads to the best results for the client. We might call it *mindful coaching*. We want to be curious and open and yet be able to regulate our attention.

In the Introduction to this book, I attempted to describe just how much is going on when you are a coach, what *being* a coach is—at least if you are going to be a good coach. In my experience, self-regulation is one of the key attributes of a good coach. And yet that is a strength that is hard to come by!

## Cultivating Healthy Curiosity as a Client

What about you?

Do you need to be curious when reading a book?

And how curious is curious enough?

What does that curiosity look and feel like?

What are you most curious about?

My most successful coaching clients are curious. Maybe not curious in the way my father was, and maybe not as curious as I am, but they are curious, nonetheless.

Most clients come to coaching because they want to change something, make sense of something, or grow in some way. And none of those things is possible without some curiosity about what is possible, some tolerance of uncertainty and periods of exploration and experimentation,

---

[7] Robert Biswas-Diener, *Positive Provocation: 25 Questions to Elevate Your Coaching Practice* (Oakland: Berrett-Koehler Publishers, 2023).

and even a general sense of excitement and discovering new ideas and techniques for doing things. Curiosity is one of the strengths I look for in clients. They don't have to have it as a superpower, but there needs to be enough to create an openness to options.

Coaching clients use curiosity to explore their options. They are curious about the following:

- What is possible for them
- How to get new opportunities
- Beliefs that get in their way or benefit them
- Learning new ways to think about old problems
- New places, roles, and people
- How to learn effectively
- Communicating effectively
- How to be a leader or manager or make a transition
- The experience of other people and their impact on those people
- What the coach knows about their current situation and what ideas the coach has seen work for other people
- What other people are thinking and why they do what they do

So, how curious are you?

What components of curiosity show up most strongly for you? And which take a back seat?

When and about what are you most curious?

## The Interaction of Client and Coach

Although coaching is generally described as "nondirective," meaning that the coach does not have their own agenda and is not steering the conversation or the outcome in a particular way, the coach still has some responsibilities.

One of those responsibilities, in my opinion, is to nurture and cultivate healthy curiosity in the client. Sometimes that means taking steps to boost the client's curiosity when they are stuck in a rut or can't think about an old problem in a new way. Or maybe their lack of curiosity about the ideas and needs of others is getting in the way of professional relationships.

At other times, the coach may challenge the client to consider whether they are being overly curious. Maybe the client's curiosity is negatively affecting some of their relationships or is getting in the way of them making an important decision.

Sometimes we are challenging the client to experiment with components of curiosity that are usually low, or we are working with them to dial back components that are causing distress.

The following table suggests some topics for each curiosity component that clients and coaches can explore together.

| COMPONENT | POTENTIAL CHALLENGES FOR THE CLIENT |
|---|---|
| High Joyous Exploration | Always looking for new ideas—doesn't follow through on choices to their conclusion. |
| | Distracted by interesting but extraneous topics. |
| | Struggles to maintain focus on stated goals. |
| Low Joyous Exploration | May get stuck in a rut or be unwilling to consider that a change of course is desirable. |
| | Not open to taking a different path or changing plans. |
| High Deprivation Sensitivity | Impatient to get on with things before doing sufficient homework. |
| | Jumps on the first solution or answer to a question or problem. |
| | Misses out on opportunities to reality check answers and get verification. |
| Low Deprivation Sensitivity | Shows no urgency to make progress. |
| | Satisfied with the status quo. |
| | May believe they know what they need to know already. |
| High Social Curiosity | Distracted by what others are doing or thinking. |
| | May get in the way of making decisions that need to be made. |
| | May cause friction with others because of perceived nosiness. |
| Low Social Curiosity | Disinclined to seek the opinions and suggestions of others. |
| | May assume that their own ideas are sufficient to move forward and that others don't have much to offer. |
| | May leave people feeling excluded or undervalued. |

| COMPONENT | POTENTIAL CHALLENGES FOR THE CLIENT |
|---|---|
| High Thrill Seeking | May be more interested in new ideas and experiences than in following something through to its conclusion. |
| | May have trouble focusing on operational and mundane work. |
| | Always seeking the best new idea or experience. |
| Low Thrill Seeking | May be resistant to change and new ideas. |
| | May like things to stay steady, even when a change is desirable. |

## Case Study: Tegan

"So, they have offered me a job back in the United States instead of in Canada." Tegan announces at the start of their next session.

The coach notices several thoughts going through her mind:

What is the job?

Where in the United States?

What happened to the role in Canada?

What does she want to do?

What about her partner?

Moving sounds exciting. How does Tegan feel?

She also notices that she feels a small sense of urgency to hear more. She wants to know more about the details, and not knowing is making her feel a little edgy.

The coach reminds herself to focus on Tegan, not on her own curiosity, and to look out for questions that might help Tegan with whatever she needs next.

As the coach sits watching Tegan, she thinks she notices changes in Tegan's expression. At first, she looks excited, then nervous, then even a little sad.

The coach asks, "I seem to see quite a few thoughts and feelings going across your face. What's happening for you now?"

Tegan takes a deep breath and answers with a list, counting off the items on her fingers as she goes along.

1. Well, first, I can't believe I didn't ask them *where* in the United States. I really am not all that bothered, but my partner was beyond

frustrated when I could not answer that question. I didn't really ask many questions at all about the logistics. I didn't feel any urgency to get all my questions answered in one sitting. It would have been overwhelming. I was happy just to hear about the role.

2. I generally think I'll get the information as I need it. This is not the first time we've moved. I'm sure we'll handle whatever happens. I suppose it would be useful to have all the details, but I can wait.

3. When we moved to South America, I was excited. It seemed like a thrilling opportunity. Now I feel tired. I am at a stage in my life where I like predictability. I guess I am turning into a stick in the mud!

4. I am curious how leadership identified this role as a possibility. I thought at this stage of my career they would give me more of the same, but this is quite a different role, setting up a new team to do new things in the organization. I wonder what the other people will be like and how they will feel about working with me. What was going through the minds of the leadership team when they decided to tap me? Maybe I'll ask to sit down with each of them and ask some questions about what their motivation was. And I wonder who else was considered for the role?

The coach takes stock for a moment, and both Tegan and the coach sit in silence.

Then the coach says slowly, "So, I heard that you are interested in the new role but not very curious about where and when it will happen. You seem confident and comfortable that you will cope with the change and that you will get the information you need as you need it. Not knowing everything right now is not distressing you. You are curious about the thinking that led to this appointment and the other people involved. And what I heard from you sounded as though this change does not feel exciting and you are not feeling much anticipation at something new. How does that sound?"

"Yeah, that's about right," Tegan answers.

"So, where do you want to start?" asks the coach.

"I would like to be more excited," Tegan blurts out. "I don't like feeling so blah about it!"

The coach pauses a moment and asks, "What would be different if you felt more excited?"

Tegan considers and then says, "I think I would have a greater sense of urgency to find out more details, and that would make my partner happier! Things have been a little tense the last few days because she does not have much to go on. If I were asking more questions, I would probably find out a lot more things I don't know yet and that would add to the excitement. I suspect I am making quite a few unfounded assumptions at the moment. And if I knew more about what is expected, I could do more to prepare. I always love that stage of a role—when it is new and there is a lot of learning to do!

When I think about the time after the move is complete, I am excited to be close to our daughter and other family. Although, of course, I really should find out where in the U.S. the job is based. We could be just as far from our daughter as we are now, come to think of it."

"So, what is your first step?" asks the coach.

"I am going to go home and work with my partner to come up with a list of questions we need answered. I think she will feel better to be part of the process, and I am pretty sure she will be relieved that I am taking it all a bit more seriously! I think we should make a list of the places we would most like to be based. They may not have mentioned a location because it might be up to me." She smiles at the thought.

"Once we have our questions, I will send the top 10 or so to the person handling the job transition and arrange a sit-down with her to find out more. Maybe I will see if I can invite my partner to join us, as she is affected by this just as much as I am, and she might like to have a firsthand opportunity to hear what is going on and to ask her own questions."

The coaching session continues, and they lay out a plan. They explore what Tegan learned from previous relocations, and they start working on a list of things that might need to be done differently this time. As Tegan leaves the session, she says, "I have a new sense of excitement and direction. I am looking forward to finding out more! Thanks!"

Our curiosity can be stifled for many reasons. For Tegan, it might be that she is generally not curious, or maybe she was feeling overwhelmed or even blindsided because this new opportunity was not what she expected. Whatever the reason, her coach helped her rekindle her curiosity, and that helped energize her. The coach also managed her own curiosity and focused on asking questions that helped Tegan decide her next moves.

Contrast that to the experience Tegan had with her friend Jamie.

Upon hearing about Tegan's new adventure, Jamie asked her the following questions (after she stopped jumping up and down and squealing):

What is the job? Tell me all about it! Is it something that you wanted? Is it related to what you are doing now?

Where in the U.S. is it? Are you going to be working in the office, or is it hybrid?

So, are you excited? You must be! I would be! How does your other half feel?

Did your daughter get excited? What did she say?

When do you leave? What do you need me to do?

You should make sure you have checked about vaccinations. And don't forget to check what you need to do to take the dog back with you!

I have a friend who specializes in international moving. I will connect the two of you. I'm sure you could use some help.

When she got home, Tegan told her "other half," "I love Jamie, but at the end of that conversation, I was exhausted! I couldn't answer one question before Jamie was asking the next one. There was no time to think! And I just felt like there was so much more to do, and yet, when I thought about it, it was not the most important stuff. And do you think I could make Jamie understand that the company provides a lot of relocation support? That would be a no!"

## Being Curious About Curiosity

Curiosity is complicated, and we have just scratched the surface. If you have more questions about curiosity, please email me for ideas about where to find out more or do some digging yourself.

Following is a set of self-reflection questions to help you explore your curiosity and how it supports you.

The next chapter will bring all the pieces together as we examine creating your meaningful life. By now, you might already be starting to see where there is already meaning. You may have made meaning out of some parts of your life and discovered meaning in others that you did not realize was there.

For those who have reached a place where meaning and purpose seem clear, the next chapter may just help solidify some of your thinking. For those of you who are still building your life of meaning, I hope you will find that Chapter 9, "Creating Your Meaningful Life: Transformation," augments what you have already discovered.

**OPTIMIZING YOUR CURIOSITY WITH SELF-COACHING QUESTIONS**

- In what ways do you want to be 5 percent more curious?
- In what ways do you want to be 5 percent less curious?
- How will you feel when you have made those adjustments?
- Which of the five components of curiosity is your strongest driver?
- Which of the five components of curiosity is least likely to drive your curiosity?
- Who do you know with higher levels of curiosity in those areas than you?
- What can you learn from them?
- When working with a coach, how curious do you want them to be?
- When your coach is personally curious about something you say, how do you want them to handle that?
- What are you most curious about after reading this chapter?
- Where will you target your curiosity tomorrow?

You can use the following charts to think through what you want in terms of curiosity from your coach. How curious do you want them to be?

The tables are reproduced here for convenience.

| PERSON | INTENSITY | FREQUENCY | DURABILITY | BREADTH | DEPTH |
|---|---|---|---|---|---|
| Coach | | | | | |
| Client | | | | | |

| PERSON | DEPRI-VATION SENSITI-VITY | JOYOUS EXPLO-RATION | STRESS TOLERANCE | SOCIAL CURIOSITY | THRILL SEEKING |
|---|---|---|---|---|---|
| Coach | | | | | |
| Client | | | | | |

One of my coaching clients said this was the balance they were looking for:

| PERSON | DEPRI-VATION SENSI-TIVITY | JOYOUS EXPLO-RATION | STRESS TOLERANCE | SOCIAL CURIOSITY | THRILL SEEKING |
|---|---|---|---|---|---|
| Coach | Low | Moderate–High | High | Moderate–High | Low |
| Client | Moderate | Moderate–High | Moderate–High | Moderate | Low |

# Moving (Closer) to Who You Want to Be

## In This Part

# Creating Your Meaningful Life: *Transformation*

> And once the storm is over, you won't remember how you made it through, how you managed to survive. You won't even be sure, whether the storm is really over. But one thing is certain. When you come out of the storm, you won't be the same person who walked in. That's what this storm's all about.
>
> —*Haruki Murakami*

We first explored the meaning of "meaning" in Chapter 1, "Finding Meaning and Purpose: Inspiration." One of the models we considered was from Michael Steger, who defined meaning as follows:

**Meaning = Coherence + Purpose + Significance**

It has taken 50 years, but I have those three components. Having them is one thing, but recognizing them is the step that opens up a world of possibility. How about you? Let's do a quick meaning check-in.

Coherence   When do you think your actions, choices, thinking, and direction are most aligned?
What are you doing?
Where are you?
Who are you with?
What are you thinking about?

Significance   When do you feel that what you are contributing is making a difference? Whether it is on a large or small scale, when do you make the biggest impact?
What are you doing?
Where are you?
Who are you with?
Who or what are you impacting?

Purpose   What is one of your medium- or long-term goals? Describe it in as much detail as you can. Engage all your senses. How does that goal feel? Where in your body do you feel it? What does that tell you? What do you visualize?
What are you doing when making progress toward your goal?
Who are you with?
Where are you?
What resources are you using—or providing?

Meaning   Review your answers to the preceding questions and then create a meaning statement that integrates the three components. Or find a quote that inspires you and captures how you feel when you are creating and finding meaning.

How do you feel now?

# Incidental Coaching

Some time ago, as I was forging my way as a program manager and sometimes speaker, a lovely lady contacted me online and asked, "What is like to be you? It must be great! To what do you attribute your success?"

I was stunned. I was flattered. And my immediate reaction was to say, "Believe me, you don't want to be me!"

Putting aside all the trite answers that would not have given her what she wanted and would not have treated her heartfelt inquiry with the respect it deserved, her question gave me great pause. In that moment, I realized that I have spent much of my life not wanting to be me. It has not been continuous, and yet as I look back, I realize there have been many times when I wished I could be someone else, be somewhere else, or have a different kind of life. And in that same moment I realized that she cannot be me and the world does not need her to be.

And I realized that I would not be me without my lifetime of experiences, that those experiences have been privileges—yes, even the uncomfortable ones. Being afraid, losing people close to me, the end of a marriage, the agonies of society seemingly tearing itself apart, poverty, oppression, even cruelty—they are all part of life's rich tapestry, as my mother would have said. Then there are the joys—the first time I held my sister the day she was born, the moments of awe-inspiring nature, the connections made with people all around the world, and moments when I get to see someone else's joy because of the progress they have made, an obstacle they have overcome, or an insight they have had.

Just writing this gives me chills!

From my father's anxiety to my grandfather's missing leg, from being accused at school of something I didn't do to lying to my parents about university, from gaining a sister at the age of nearly 6 instead of remaining an only child. From struggling with anxiety to doing things anyway. From growing up in one neighborhood to moving 24 times in recent years. From marriage to divorce. From deciding not to have children to adopting two. Every nook and cranny of my life has shaped who I am today and what is happening to me now, and what will happen in the future will continue to shape and reshape me.

If I had made different choices, gone to different places, or grown up in a different household, I would have been entirely different. Without a sister there is a whole side of my life I would not have experienced. The list goes on.

Suddenly, I had found my sense of meaning, as clear as day. Meaning, for me, comes from learning, growing, and sharing. It involves taking each experience and looking for how it can enhance me. For me, personal growth is meaning, supporting others is meaning, and being connected to the world is meaning.

## Is Meaning Found or Created?

And this brings me back to the question I asked at the start of the book.

Do we find meaning, or do we create meaning?

Do we make choices that bring us in line with a life that we predefine as meaningful?

Or, do we experience life and learn from each experience, treating what happens and how we respond as lessons to learn?

We all transform, whether we intend to or not, whether we notice it as it happens or not. We are neither the same as we were nor are we exactly what we expected we would be.

The word *transformation* has powerful connotations. It suggests change, and not just any change but dramatic, extensive change that makes the new form almost unrecognizable from the original form.

Think about who you are now and ask yourself what the you of 20 years ago would say about the new you. There are some questions at the end of the chapter to help you.

Imagine the younger you walking around the current you as though you are on display. The younger you looks you up and down and evaluates your appearance. They laugh at your hair, are surprised at your choice of outfit, and, as they look over your resume and your social media accounts, they marvel at the things you have gone on to do—and be—since they last knew you. Maybe they are shocked at some of your current beliefs or astonished at some of your passions.

Some of what you have done they had not even imagined. Other things the younger you had considered and ruled out as impossible—or at least unlikely. Yet other things the younger you planned for and anticipated doing and being have not yet come to pass, and some of those ideas are barely remembered and are certainly no longer on the radar or bucket list of the older you.

For many of us, our younger self seeing our older self today would say, "Wow, what a transformation!" Hopefully that transformation is positive, and we are more than our younger self thought possible. Sometimes the opposite is true, and our younger self is dismayed at how things turned out.

There are three ways we influence this lifelong process of transformation. All three ways come into play for each of us. The choice we make concerns the balance between chance and intent, reaction and choice, and whether our journey is solitary or collaborative.

1. We can leave it to chance, meaning that we experience our experiences, react and respond to them, and, over time, those experiences and our responses result in semi-permanent changes in how we behave, think, and feel.

2. We can be intentional in the experiences we choose and the way we respond to experiences thrust upon us. We can clearly identify our values and make decisions guided by what we know.

3. We can get help. We can work with others to identify what is possible, to challenge our own habitual thinking, and to explore

possibilities that alone we may just not see and certainly don't consider as serious options. Other people help us look beyond the obvious and create transformations that would otherwise be out of our reach.

When I chose the quote at the beginning of this chapter, it was because of the idea of a storm. Storms are usually thrust upon us, often without notice. Life is filled with stormy moments, and as difficult as they may be, they test us and provide opportunities to discover aspects about ourselves that the quiet moments do not. The question is how we approach these storms. Do we struggle through them alone, or do we enlist help along the way?

I—and my clients, it seems—believe we uncover more insights and discover them more quickly when we work with a coach. They help us get further, faster!

## Discoveries You Would Have Made Anyway—Eventually

In a recent coaching chemistry session, a short meeting where I and a potential coaching client meet to discuss coaching options and assess our compatibility, I was asked the following three questions:

"How long does coaching take?"

"Does coaching really change anything?"

"What does coaching do that I could not do for myself?"

The answers to these questions are not always satisfying to the potential client because as a coach, I cannot guarantee anything other than that I will do the best I can, bring my best coaching skills to your aid, and that I will strive to enhance and tailor those skills as we go along. The only other thing I can guarantee is that if you are prepared to work at least moderately hard, something will happen—something will change.

How long does it take? Well, that depends on the purpose, you, the work you put in, and the environment around you. Some coaching topics can be tackled quickly, whereas others take more time to peel back the layers of the onion and even to fully define the challenge at hand. Is my client really here to come up with a time management plan, or is the underlying topic for coaching the things they are telling themselves that make time management more of a challenge than it needs to be? Are we here to come up with a schedule or to explore the running commentary in the client's head? Or, are we here to do some combination of those and maybe some other things along the way?

Does coaching really change anything? Transformation starts with developing and increasing self-awareness. While some people have great self-awareness—or at least think they do—research shows that we all tend to be myopic when it comes to self-awareness.[1] We generally believe we have higher levels of self-awareness than we do. And often we believe people around us are sadly lacking in self-awareness.

I am not only referring to the self-awareness to recognize the choices and behaviors we adopt, but also the self-awareness needed to distinguish between symptoms and underlying causes. A symptom of the way we talk to ourselves may be that we are always late for things. No matter how hard we try, we just cannot seem to get where we are going on time. We think we have a time management problem. That is the symptom.

Once we start digging deeper, we discover that we are giving ourselves unhelpful messages that *result* in rarely being on time.

I will save the last question—"What does coaching do that I cannot do for myself?"—until after the following case study.

## Case Study: Jamal

Jamal is late again. The coaching session was scheduled for 10 a.m., and at 10:05 a.m., the coach is still the only one in the room. Finally, Jamal enters.

"Sorry I am late," he says. "Actually, that is what I want explore today—ways to manage my time better."

The coach waits and Jamal continues.

"I have always been late to everything. It just seems to be who I am. My mother always says I am undisciplined. I think it is because I get distracted easily. I am getting ready to do something and some other activity catches my attention and before I know it, I am running behind. It starts as soon as I get up. I pick up my phone. Some of what I do with the phone is for me. That is when I read some news and check the weather. Often that is when I message close friends and family and generally check in.

[1] Tasha Eurich, "What Self-Awareness Really Is (and How to Cultivate It)," Harvard Business Review, accessed April 6, 2023, https://hbr.org/2018/01/what-self-awareness-really-is-and-how-to-cultivate-it

"Then one thing leads to another, and I am checking email. Have you ever seen the statistics that your phone captures. Scary! The amount of time I spend on my phone is ridiculous. But I cannot do without it. I could not function. These days we all have to carry our phones with us at all times, don't we?" Jamal smiles, expecting the coach to agree.

"Who says?" asks the coach.

Jamal looks startled and for a moment struggles to find the words to explain how strange that question is. Each time he seems to formulate a response, he dismisses it. After a few seconds, he gathers himself and starts to list the reasons having the phone close by is essential.

"Clients want to get in touch about project setbacks and emergencies. If I had not had my phone on Monday, my client would not have been able to tell me before 9 a.m. that the delivery they were expecting was late, and it would have been another day before it arrived. Instead, I was able to chase it up, and it was delivered at 4:30 p.m. that same day! Of course, dealing with that problem made me late to my first meeting. And, come to think of it, we still had to wait until the next day to get started on the next phase of the project. . ."

Jamal searches for other reasons and comes up with a short list of candidates:

1. I might miss something important!

2. People might be frustrated or annoyed when they cannot reach me.

3. My mother, for example, would be upset if she couldn't reach me whenever she needed to.

4. And clients need to be able to let me know they are running late, changing a meeting, etc.

5. I keep my to-do lists on my phone, and those are the only things that keep me on track for appointments.

Jamal seems to settle on the impact on other people as a compelling reason.

"Yes, people would be annoyed if I did not have my phone with me."

"And. . ." the coach says quietly.

Again, Jamal looks surprised.

"And. . . and. . ." Jamal is lost for words.

Then he continues, "And nothing, I suppose. The world won't end. I am not a brain surgeon. People would wait and, in all likelihood, they would just move on to the next thing."

"So what do you want to explore further?" the coach asks.

"I think I need to consider the unhelpful things I tell myself. If I didn't believe I have be at everyone's beck and call and think that it's an obligation to always be accessible by phone, I would have more space to think, plan, get things done, and, well, be on time!"

So what do you think? "What does coaching do that I cannot do for myself?"

The answer is multifaceted.

In principle, Jamal could have come to that discovery himself. Maybe with the help of his mother, friends, or by finding a great YouTube video. He might have used self-reflection and introspection to spot the self-talk supporting the behavior. And he might not have. Chances are, even if he did get to the same point, it would have taken a lot longer to get there.

# And Discoveries That Might Have Remained Hidden

For some people, the advantage of having a coach is speed. Could my client I mentioned earlier accomplish the same result as we did together in 20 minutes? Maybe. Although she had been trying for months.

And for others, introspection is not enough. The input and support of friends and family does not result in new possibilities but more of the same.

Sometimes, coaching can lead to discoveries you might never have made on your own—and the pathways to even more transformation are opened up as a result.

## Sometimes It Is About Recognition

Another quote from Haruki Murakami that I considered using at the start of this chapter was "Sometimes it's not the people who change, it's the mask that falls off."

I love that quote as a coach because as often as our clients are changing from who they have been to who they want to be, just as often they are changing from who they have been molded to be into who they always had the potential to be. The transformation is not just in the person but in their self-perception.

Pause for a moment and consider what and who has influenced you to be the person you are today. What are some expectations of others that have nudged you in one direction or another?

My parents were the first in their generation to go to college. Their expectation was that I would go to college—and that it would be a "better" college than the one they attended. Their dream was that I would attend either Cambridge or Oxford. The course of study did not matter to them—in fact, they assumed universities as prestigious as Oxford and Cambridge would have all the majors I could possibly want to consider.

My girls' school had a great track record of educating girls and helping them succeed in a world where academic success was expected much more of boys than girls—especially in STEM subjects. They were eager to see me succeed, and they too measured my success by the university to which I was accepted. They were all in for me getting a Cambridge or Oxford education.

My father was scientist. My mother loved art, literature, and people. She worked in social work, probation, and child and family services. Anytime I had a chance to go to my father's office, I would jump at it. The people always loved to greet the children of colleagues, and there were always fun experiments to play with (some of which my playing messed up).

Similarly, I loved helping my mother. On rare occasions, I was able to accompany her to help people who were struggling in one way or another. I helped one family move to a new house. The father had lost a leg in a workplace accident and couldn't carry things easily. Another time, I tutored a girl in math. Another time, I helped teach some children at my mom's clinic how to read. In college, my professor asked me to help someone in passing her exams well enough to overcome the failing grade she had received on a term essay due to inadvertent plagiarism.

Obviously, I was a scientist, right? I was influenced by school and family to pursue scientific pursuits—math, physics, and chemistry. My father was dismayed when I got a grade A in art but only a B in chemistry. My father wanted me to read wise texts and scientific papers—and I did. But in the evenings, my mother and I read classic literature aloud and listened to the daily story on Woman's Hour on the radio. My father only grudgingly accepted the art in Shakespeare when he had to help me pass my school exams and to do so he deigned to take me to a modern style performance of *Julius Caesar*. My love for live performance was born.

I loved science, and yet I was always drawn to people.

I became an accountant, but I was bored out of my mind. I applied to study math at university, but I was turned down because of pesky exam results. I turned to economics—scientific enough for my father (just about) and enjoyable because of the application of math—but I could not sustain any interest in any aspect of economic theory except the behavioral side. I became a project manager, largely because I was organized, focused, and a problem solver. And yet my first project management role resulted from the relationship I already had with the client. As my project management career blossomed, my interests turned to troubled projects, team motivation, team conflict resolution, and effective communication.

And then, after building a solid career in project management, I burned out. That is a story for another time. But that burnout resulted in a transformation. Just as the question from the lady online unmasked my sense of meaning, so that burnout fostered not a change, but another unmasking.

Finally, with help of a coach, I was able to reconsider who I am at my core. Yes, I love science. Yes, I am curious. Yes, I am shy. Yes, I love spending time alone. Yes, I love to unravel scientific mysteries and build solutions from the resources on hand. (I have been known to be quite the MacGyver![2])

In a coaching session one day, I stated with confidence, "I am not a people person."

My coach looked at me quizzically and asked, "What is a people person?"

My second unmasking had begun!

## Being Clear About the Value of Transformation

The following are three of the favorite questions of many coaches:

1.  How will making a change benefit you?
2.  What will happen if you don't make that change?
3.  How is the current situation serving you?

These questions invite the client to consider the incentive to change. Many of us want to be different. Taller, thinner, smarter, more popular, happier—the list goes on. However, wanting it and being willing to do what it takes to make it so are not the same thing.

So, before you and your coach spend precious time on a fruitless endeavor, it is important to explore your level of commitment to that transformation.

Each of the preceding questions asks you to look forward and predict, albeit imperfectly, possible outcomes.

---

[2] Not familiar with the U.S. colloquialism of a "MacGyver"? Find out more at https://en.wikipedia.org/wiki/MacGyver

If you are successful in transforming, what will the future look like? Chapter 5, "Being Hopeful: Expectation," explored hope. The first step was to visualize the result or a waypoint on the journey. Without that visualization, it is hard to create the motivation and impetus to make change. It is the first stage of building hope. Once you have articulated how things will be better, you and your coach can start to identify pathways and decide what steps you can and will take to make the outcome you want more likely.

By contrast, it is good to consider what life will be like if things stay the same. This can either give you comfort that to try and not succeed is okay or can be part of the incentive to make changes. If your alternative future is not one you want, that may help inspire and energize you.

The third question is a tough one—and in many ways the most important. If you have an end in mind and know at least some of the steps you need to take to achieve it but are not taking those steps, then something must be making the current situation preferable.

Clients bring many examples:

1. A client who wants to leave a relationship does not want to experience the guilt and discomfort of telling someone they are not the person anymore. Peace and quiet, predictability, and maintaining the status quo for their partner and family feels easier to deal with than the uncertainty of change and the risk that others will judge them harshly or cut them off.

2. A client who has long held a dream of launching a business on their own has not taken the step of quitting their current full-time job even though they have set up their new company, identified the target market, and even identified their first two clients. They are used to a certain standard of living and are afraid that if their new business falters, they and their family will be uncomfortable. It is more comfortable to ensure their safety and comfort than to take the chance that the new business won't work out.

3. A stay-at-home mother whose children have left for college, and who has been thinking about going back to school to continue her training as a nurse, has not visited possible schools or registered for classes. She loved nursing when she was young, but her training was interrupted when she had the first of her three children. She tells herself that with all the new technology now, she would be overwhelmed, and that she would struggle to be on her feet all day. She gets pleasure from thinking about what might be and is afraid to be disappointed.

These are just some of the situations my clients have encountered. And coaching can help untangle the myth from reality, the concerns that justify action, and the ones that are unhelpful self-talk. With a coach, you get to reality check your beliefs, consider what safety nets might be available, and truly understand the value of change.

The answer to each of these questions is not a foregone conclusion. Sometimes the current situation may be the better one. We may discover that the first client is dissatisfied with more things than their relationship and that they may have other routes to happiness. Or we may discover in coaching that while the risks are real, they are worth it. Or we may identify another path that makes more sense and gives the same relief— for example, one of my clients got a job that involved more travel. Suddenly their relationship with their significant other seemed a lot more fun and interesting.

The second client might discover things that make success in their new venture unlikely and that a different direction makes sense. Or maybe there are resources the client can explore that will reduce the risk. Or, perhaps they have done their homework and have minimized the risks, and have realized that the opportunity is worth it to get closer to who they really are. For example, I had a client who investigated local grants and business launch programs and found they were eligible for numerous forms of financial and professional assistance. That gave them a safety net that made taking the entrepreneurial leap less risky.

For the third client, maybe the dream of being a nurse will turn out not to be the best goal. Or maybe she will discover that her reservations, while natural, are not reasons to stop her from at least finding out more about the nursing school. After all, even if she decides against nursing, she might find something else to pursue. For example, one client who was considering going back to her previous career realized that what she wanted was to feel useful and to be able to interact with others. She retrained as a coach-counselor and became a school student advisor.

And that brings me to another aspect of transformation.

## Being Open to Surprises

Some of the biggest transformations I see in friends, family, and clients come from unexpected sources.

I did not think I would burn out and realize I was done with project management as my profession. But that moment when my declining mental health became apparent to all was a reset. In less than 6 months,

I was building my skills and passion for coaching; I was working on a book with a publisher; and I was speaking in front of audiences about my burnout experience.

A friend and her husband decided they wanted to start a family. Both were what people would generally call type A personalities—competitive, driven, determined. They showed the same determination in planning for their new arrival.

Then the baby came. They were not ready for what happened to them. They transformed from assertive businesspeople who were always on the road into homebodies who took enormous pleasure in creating a growth environment for their child. Now business was about getting enough rather than getting more. They focused on creating wealth through experiences rather than through the accumulation of money and things.

At the other end of the spectrum, a client whose last child was going off to college was convinced that being an empty nester would be intolerable. As a single parent, his daily routine was built around the activities of his children. Their mother had died 12 years prior. His work was a way of making enough money; he had no real career aspirations. Their house was laid out with family living in mind. When the first two children left home to attend college, he enjoyed focusing his attention on his youngest. Now he would be flying solo.

The first few weeks were challenging. He felt a little lost and purposeless. Then, on week four, he came to coaching excited. Several things had happened.

First, he had stayed at work late one night—no longer feeling the need to rush home—and had struck up a conversation about a new role that was opening. He had decided to apply for it, which would mean a promotion and leadership training.

Then, while he was speaking with his sister on the phone, she reminded him that as a young man he loved to sing. He researched choirs in the area and decided to join one. Not only did he enjoy getting back to singing, but he enjoyed meeting new people.

The sister of one of my clients found herself caught in an attack on her country by a neighboring country. The world was turned upside down for her, her family, and friends. In an instant, she had to start making decisions about how to ensure the safety of herself and her family. She discovered that under pressure she is clear-headed and decisive. She had expected that such a traumatic event would leave her bewildered and lost, that she would be unable to think clearly when under so much pressure. Instead, she found that she was able to be bewildered and still make choices. She and her family quickly decided to leave the country—at least temporarily. And she ended up using her experiences to counsel others going through similar upheavals.

And the biggest surprises can come in coaching. Sometimes a magical moment occurs when the coach asks a question that seems to move the client's perspective by 90 degrees, and they see the world and their options in new ways.

Or there is a moment when the coach invites the client to explore what has changed and the client gets to see all the incremental changes and how they are adding up to that transformation.

## Coaches Transform Too

As I prepared to write this chapter, I reflected on my own transformation. I looked back on the shy girl who was afraid of everything when she was young. She was a "good girl" who did the things her parents, teachers, and society expected. Growing up in the United Kingdom, my experiences were subtly different from those of children in the United States. The expectations may have been different as well.

I also compared the coach I was as a project manager with the coach I became when I participated in my earliest training. I thought about how my assumption that I would be exclusively a 1:1 coach transformed when I first experienced leading group coaching sessions during the pandemic. My coaching has been transformed by technology, by the spread of online services and tools, and by extraordinary teachers. And the best teachers of all have been my clients. The more clients I meet, the more I learn about coaching. And the more I learn, the more I want to learn—and share.

And the more I learn and share, the more I transform. I recommend adding a question to your coaching chemistry session. Ask your coach how they have and are transforming!

## Some Last Thoughts on Meaning and Transformation

Writing this book has transformed me. It has changed who I am in relation to the world. It has changed my relationship with coaching and clients. It has changed my relationship with my book advisors and with you. And that transformation feels meaningful to me.

Hopefully, reading this book has transformed you too—maybe in a big way, maybe in incremental ways. What you decide to do—or not do—today is likely to take you further along on your pathway of transformation. So, choose wisely!

Choose experiences, actions, and thoughts that advance your purpose, and when you have unexpected experiences, take time to reflect and learn from them.

And above all, use your experiences to be *you*. The world needs you. The visual shows the relationship of meaning to the topics of the book's chapters.

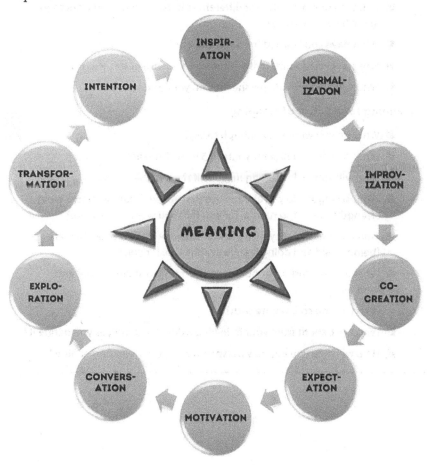

## REFLECTING ON YOUR TRANSFORMATION

- What are three things you wanted to accomplish 20 years ago that you laugh at now?

- What are three experiences you have had that the younger you would have thought impossible or beyond your reach?

- What are three things you have accomplished that the younger you would be impressed by?

- What are three things on your horizon that were beyond the realms of your imagination when you were younger?

- What are three aspirations of your younger self that you would like to rekindle as goals?

- What are the three biggest differences between who you were then and who you are now?

- What have you learned from this exercise?

- What will you do differently tomorrow because of this exercise?

- Who will help provide perspective on your journey so far?

### Planning for a Sense of Meaning

- What do you want your epitaph to say?

- What do you visualize for yourself 5 years from now?

- Who will you be impacting most in life?

- What strengths do you already use that you will lean on more? What strengths are not so natural for you that you want to cultivate?

- Think of times when you are brave. What conditions make bravery (being afraid and doing it anyway) possible for you?

- What are you curious about in the short term, medium term, and long term?

- Who will you collaborate with?

- Who will benefit from your following a life of meaning as you define it?

- Who will help you get new perspective on your plan for meaning?

CHAPTER

# 10

# Conclusion: Choosing Your Next Act: *Intention*

> When I dare to be powerful—to use my strength in the service of my vision, then it becomes less and less important whether I am afraid.
>
> —*Audre Lorde*

Thank you for sticking with me this far. I hope you agree that you have come on quite a journey since starting this book and that you see you already have many tools in your toolbox.

At the start, I said we were going to explore the following topics:

Finding meaning & purpose: *inspiration*

In your own way: *normalization*

Getting out of your own way: *improvisation*

Appreciating the coaching journey: *co-creation*

Being hopeful: *expectation*

Being strong: *motivation*

Being brave: *conversation*

Being curious: *exploration*

Creating your meaningful life: *transformation*

This chapter concludes the book with some thoughts about where we have been and where we are going. I encourage you to leave this book with intention.

## Revisiting Being Open to Surprises

This book came about because Kenyon Brown, an acquisitions editor at John Wiley, started following me on social media. After a few weeks of interaction, he messaged me and asked if we could have a conversation. Without hesitation, I agreed, and we set up a call.

After a brief and surprising conversation, Kenyon asked me to work with him on a book proposal. Unlike other coaching books, its purpose would not be to advise coaches on how to be more effective coaches; rather, its audience would be the people who could benefit from coaching and who hesitate to try it. It would be for the people who didn't yet know what coaching is and how it works. It would be for the people who wanted to peek behind the curtain of coaching to find out more. And it would be for people who wanted to get started right away, who would consider working with a coach, and at the same time, hope there were things they could do on their own to kickstart learning and growth.

There are multiple models of coaching. None of them suits everyone; all of them offer something useful.

This model is based on the work I have done with clients individually and in groups from across the world. It is built on a foundation of research, training, and personal experience as a coach and a client. And it is bolstered by the wise advice and input of fellow coaches, willing clients, and impactful teachers.

So, surprise number one was to be invited to propose this book.

Surprise number two was how much writing this book clarified my beliefs about coaching, challenged my assumptions, and heightened my passion for the art, science, and magic of coaching.

Surprise number three was that my life is *full* of meaning. It is not perfect, but it is fulfilling. It is not always smooth sailing, but I have resources and friends, and I can cope. There is wind in my sails, and my hull is sound!

Finally, surprise number four was how important every life experience has been and continues to be. We really are the total of every experience to date.

I am living proof that hope, strengths, bravery, and curiosity are good foundations for finding and building a sense of meaning.

## Surprises Invite Us to Take a Fresh Perspective

Writing a book is a rollercoaster. Once the initial excitement diminishes, the work begins. There are times when it seems impossible to formulate ideas in a useful way. And there are times when the ideas seem to flow faster than you can find the words to capture them.

About a third of the way through writing this book, I had an epiphany. Although from the outside it probably seemed sudden, it had been coming for months. The work I did on the early chapters about inspiration, normalization, and improvisation helped me see with absolute clarity that I needed to live in a different environment. As beautiful as the beach is, I need something else. I need a bustling center of activity and inspiration. I need a community aligned with what I am doing and being.

So, my husband and I started co-creating a solution. He proposed that we move and started researching places to move to. We reached out to people we knew who could help make it happen. We had a lot of brave conversations and explored ways we could make a change that worked for us both. We spent many long days building a workable plan.

We sold our house, found a new home, arranged a temporary rental, and packed our belongings. And with a lot of expectation and motivation, we were ready to move.

Then, about five days before we were scheduled to move, we had another surprise. As we savored the prospect of a new chapter in our lives, a favorite song came on the radio. My husband held out his hand and asked, "May I have this dance?" For various reasons we have not danced in a long time, so this invitation made me smile. I stood up and took his hand, and we began to dance slowly around the living room.

As the music reached its conclusion, my husband did something uncharacteristically "wild." He dipped me. And that is when it happened: I slipped, he tripped, and we landed on the floor in an ungainly heap with my leg pinned beneath him. As he disentangled himself, we stared in dismay at my right leg. There was no way that my foot would normally be in that position. My doctor told me, "No weight-bearing *at all*" on that leg for 6–10 weeks, depending on the surgery.

## Taking Stock

Both of us had to take stock. We had to answer the questions of how to get two cars to our new location and how to manage the move when I was incapacitated. The questions and challenges came thick and fast, yet I could not help but see how lucky I am. I have the resources to get good treatment; I live in a country where treatment is available; and I have a position in society that does not put additional obstacles in the way of getting treatment. We are both resourceful and have the mindset that every problem has a solution. I have a husband who is able, willing, and similarly resourceful. (I could write a whole book about his resourcefulness!)

I have a community that is supportive, responsive, encouraging, empowering, and, above all, kind. The offers of help came quickly. People rallied around me. I felt so supported, as did my husband.

## Being Hopeful

We reevaluated our short-term goals and co-created a clear vision of what success over the next few days, weeks, and months would look like. Once we had that clear vision, we looked at ways to achieve it, including options we would never usually consider. We hired someone to take my car to the new location on a flatbed truck instead of having to worry about how to get two cars and a trailer from the coast to the middle of the state.

And we started to make lists and assign tasks to make it more likely that things would work out as we envisioned.

I did more of the logistics, making phone calls, ensuring that we had the services we needed. I coordinated with the movers and changed the parameters of the contract so that they did more packing and we did less. My husband started packing and loading. We had other setbacks; the stiflingly hot weather meant the move had to be delayed—the moving team had heat exhaustion! Throughout the process, we maintained our belief that we can adapt, we can cope, and that no challenge was insurmountable.

## Being Strong

Since I first started studying strengths of character, my husband and I have become well aware of our own strengths. We know that our strengths sometimes cause friction—for example, we are both high in fairness but have a different understanding of what fairness is. I am a doer and tend to learn as I go along. I start a task and adjust as I go, whereas my husband wants a full end-to-end plan. He is extraordinarily high in critical thinking and has a very detail-oriented mind. I have to remember to keep my patience with his meticulous process, just as he has to remind himself that I like to move fast.

I used my strength of gratitude to help me focus on what we were accomplishing and not dwell on things that might be slipping through the cracks. I used appreciation of beauty to create space for myself, taking time to get outside and enjoy our surroundings. My husband used his ingenuity and creativity to come up with novel and unexpected ways of solving problems as we went along.

## Being Brave

From the conversation when I first raised my desire to be in a different location, we had difficult conversations. Our priorities don't always exactly match, and there were many times when we had to compromise. We focused on giving and taking equally rather than always deciding on the middle ground when we disagreed.

It took bravery to not settle for solutions that left each of us unsatisfied but instead taking turns to relinquish control or put aside a personal preference so the other person could be wholly satisfied.

My husband arranged our travel plans. Some of his choices were not my first choice by any means, but as he was the only person who could drive us and he was doing 99 percent of the work to ensure that we had what we needed at the rental house, I agreed that we would arrange the travel the way he wanted.

Other times, we were brave enough to stand our ground and make clear that something was nonnegotiable.

It was often uncomfortable, but we had the conversations and made the hard decisions anyway.

## Being Curious

Both of us are extraordinarily curious. My husband has a passion for science, discovery, and the unknown, such as space, and he likes to have the questions answered before he acts. I am curious about people, situations, and the world and its interactions. I only need to satisfy enough curiosity to get started on the next task. I trust that we will work things out as we go.

We got curious about how bones heal. We got curious about what equipment might help in this situation. I asked a friend and colleague who uses a wheelchair to help me understand where to focus my attention on navigating challenges in my mobility and strength.

As tiring as the whole transition was, we treated it as an adventure. We learned a lot!

# Moving Forward with Intention—and Action

As we come to the end of this part of your journey, let's think about the way forward. What is your intention now?

And what action will you take now?

How will what we have explored help you to move forward?

This section discusses intentions, habits, and actions. We are going to look at intentions in the short, medium, and long term. But what do those timeframes mean? That is your first decision.

Many of my project management colleagues use a 30-day to 60-day to 90-day planning horizon. Although there are general goals (intentions) that go beyond those timeframes, oftentimes in a project, 90 days is the maximum time period that can be successfully planned in detail with sufficient certainty to make such planning appropriate and useful.

Look in other places, and you will find people talking about medium-term goals as 1–3 years, and long-term goals as 10 years or more.

Let's start with the simplest idea: immediate intentions.

## Immediate Intention

When you are going to do or be something different, there is no time like the present! Change starts as soon as you start changing! Now that you have finished the book, what is one thing you will do differently starting today?

Not tomorrow, not next week, not when you are "less busy" or "more settled" or have a new job, or when you get fit. Now.

My mother's favorite proverb was, "The road to Hell is paved with good intentions."

Setting your intention is important; otherwise, you won't know where you are trying to go or recognize when you get there. But an intention is only the start. Choose an action and act on it as soon as possible.

## Habit Forming and Building

> Humans are creatures of habit. If you quit when things get tough, it gets that much easier to quit the next time. On the other hand, if you force yourself to push through it, the grit begins to grow in you.
>
> —*Travis Bradberry*

Ingrained, repeatable habits don't happen overnight. Creating a new habit can be very difficult; it takes time and repetition. One of the things we are likely to experience is lapses in our new habit, so a foundational habit we want to cultivate is to stay the course, even if we have turned off for a day or two.

### First Foundational Habit: Return to the Plan

If you are trying to eat healthier food, exercise four days a week, read more, and call your friends and family regularly, there will be days, maybe even weeks, when you will skip the gym, snack on unhealthful food, fall asleep before you get that chapter read, and forget to call your parents. And that is okay.

The number one habit to cultivate is to return to the habit as soon as you can. There is no shame in falling out of the new routine, but you are being your own worst enemy if you let falling out of the routine mean giving up the routine.

### Second Foundational Habit: Regularly Review the Value of the Habit You Are Trying to Set

Just because you decide to do something differently, it does not mean the new way is the best way—for you. Remember to evaluate whether your new diet is working the way you want. How are your energy levels? How are you sleeping? Are you enjoying the exercise when you do it? What other forms of exercise might be more enjoyable and therefore easier to maintain?

### Third Foundational Habit: Build in Milestone Celebrations

One of the things I see most often in coaching is that we forget to savor our progress. Often, we don't even notice the progress we have made. And if we don't notice our progress, it is all the harder to maintain!

## Medium-Term Intention

Imagine that it is 3–6 months from now. We are walking toward each other on the street, and we recognize each other. We stop, and after exchanging the usual niceties (which is a habit by the way), I ask you, "What are you consistently doing—or being—that changed after you read the book?"

What do you want your answer to be?

With that in mind, write down the first step you will take—immediately. What will you do differently today that will move you closer to being able to tell me good news?

What habits will you put in place to make the outcome more likely?

What will you change if this new habit is elusive?

How will you measure your progress toward your 3-month goal?

What milestones will you use? How will you reward yourself as you build the habit?

See you in 3 months! I look forward to hearing good news from you.

## Long-Term Intention

Maybe your long-term horizon is the end of the quarter, the end of the year, or 1–3 years from now. Maybe it is 10 years from now. Whatever the horizon, that is fine. Be sure you are clear about what each time horizon is for you. It is important for measuring progress and identifying when change is necessary.

We meet in a few months' time. You report that you kicked off your changes on day one, you have navigated lapses, and you returned to your new routines. You have made progress—not always at the pace you wanted, but progress nonetheless. I suggest a check-in when you are reaching your long-term horizon. You get to choose the timing. What do you choose? When do you want to meet?

The following table shows some sample time horizons. These are based on observation.

| TYPE | IMMEDIATE-TERM | HABITS | MEDIUM-TERM | LONG-TERM |
|---|---|---|---|---|
| **Personal** | Today | Next 1–3 months | 1 month | 3–6 months |
| **Professional** | Next 30 days | 60–90 days | 3–6 months | 1–3 years |
| **Family** | 3–9 months | 1–10 years | 5–15 years | 15–25 years |

| TYPE | IMMEDIATE-TERM | HABITS | MEDIUM-TERM | LONG-TERM |
|---|---|---|---|---|
| **Community** | 1–3 years | 1–5 years | 3–7 years | 7–15 years |
| **Society (U.S.)** | 1–4 years | Variable | 5–15 years | 15–40 years |

And here is a blank table that you can use to fill in your own numbers:

| TYPE | IMMEDIATE-TERM | HABITS | MEDIUM-TERM | LONG-TERM |
|---|---|---|---|---|
| **Personal** | | | | |
| **Professional** | | | | |
| **Family** | | | | |
| **Community** | | | | |
| **Society (U.S.)** | | | | |

# Launch Your Meaningful Life

With the tools of hope, strengths, bravery, and curiosity, you have what you need to overcome what is usually the biggest obstacle to a life of flourishing and meaning—you. By using the science of hope, you gain not just a vision of your possible future but put plans in place to get there.

With your strengths (and the strengths of those around you), you get to see the resources you already have. More than knowing what you have available, you learn to dial them up and down, call on others, and develop constellations of strengths that enhance and balance each other.

By first recognizing ways in which you are already brave, understanding what bravery is, and by understanding that you can tolerate more than you think you can, you create a mindset that extends your comfort zone and puts more things within your reach.

And with curiosity, you have a powerful tool for developing, growing, and embracing even unpleasant experiences as opportunities. Be curious about the people you meet, the places you visit, and the opportunities and setbacks that come your way, and learn to leverage every experience for your own good.

I look forward to hearing your stories!

You have what you need to go a long way, so over to you.

Be hopeful, be strong, be brave, and be curious!

# Afterword—AI: Next-Level Coaching or Ethical No-no?

---

**An idea that is not dangerous is unworthy of being called an idea at all.**

*—Oscar Wilde*

---

Coaching is always evolving.

As I started to work on this book, we had reached another milestone in human history: A new generation of machine "thinking" was being unleashed. The latest iteration of artificial intelligence (AI), in the form of online tools such as Bard, ChatGPT, and more, was causing a flurry of interest, activity, debate, and more than a little consternation.

My first reaction was to stay well away. I found it hard to wrap my head around the idea of a machine "thinking." It has been a long time since computers were first able to win at chess, come up with the best routes to our destination, or even control our living environment. But I don't want my computer deciding I am better off having my house at a higher or lower temperature or that the route it wants me to take in the car is the only acceptable one.

Now, we were faced with an incarnation of AI that could be confused with us. How will we know if essays, articles, entry examinations, bar exams, and more have been created by a human, by AI, or by some combination of both? How will our coaches know we are human?

As a huge fan of *Lost in Space* back in the 1960s, all I could hear in my head was the robot's voice warning, "Danger, Will Robinson." For those who don't remember the original *Lost in Space* TV show or who have only seen the recent remake, the robot was cunningly called "Robot."

My sense of danger was and is a vague unease—a feeling that this won't end well. However, I cannot really say specifically why I feel this way. I suspect that in the early 1800s, I would have been a Luddite, suspicious of "newfangled machinery" that could do things for, or more importantly, to or instead of us.

But hasn't every technological advance given us pause? And hasn't every technological advance been a mixed blessing with some unintended consequences—both positive and negative?

When my mother got her first front-loading washing machine, my two grandmothers pulled up chairs to watch as the clothes spun around. The comments alternated between a barely audible, "What will they think of next?" and a much louder exclamation of, "Why do we need this anyway? What is wrong with a twin tub, a mangle, and a Mackeson's?" In fact, at one point, my maternal grandmother even asked, "Well, when will a woman drink her Mackeson's now?" (The tradition at the time was that many women would drink a bottle of Mackeson Stout or Guinness while doing the laundry to supplement the amount of iron and vitamins they were consuming.)

When I was dating my first boyfriend, we spent hours talking on the phone. My mother would ask, "What is wrong with a letter?" or "Why don't you get on your bike and actually meet in person somewhere?"

When the Internet arrived, my mother said, "I cannot imagine this will catch on!"

Suddenly, confronted with AI, I turned into my grandmothers and became deeply wary.

---

**At this moment in time, I confess to burying my head in the sand on all things AI. It just makes me feel. . .yuck. There may be a place for AI in coaching, but I'm not quite ready for it!**

*—Asila Calhoun, Leadership Coach & Principal, Calhoun Consulting*

---

A few weeks later, I was participating with my entrepreneurial women's mentoring/support group. Our amazing organizer, Crystal Richards, said, "Has anyone been using AI? Isn't it amazing?"

Immediately, the energy level in the virtual room began to rise and people started to exchange their experiences, their rating of one tool over another, and discuss the merits—or lack thereof—of AI in their field.

I sat in silence, a little dismayed. Everyone was so excited, but all I could see was the beginning of the end of the world.

## Case Study: Tegan

When the screen came on, Tegan was looking away, deep in conversation with someone on another screen. Her sound was muted.

The coach waited, reminding herself to confirm that this was still a good time and that Tegan was in a quiet place. After all, it seemed as though people might be around who could hear their session.

At last Tegan turned back. She smiled shyly and said, "Sorry, I was just following up on a meeting summary with my assistant."

The coach was surprised. Tegan had never mentioned having an assistant, even though the topic of overwork and bureaucracy had come up often!

Before the coach could decide whether it would be appropriate to ask more about it, Tegan said, "Actually, it's a virtual assistant. It's an avatar. I get to choose its appearance, gender, ethnicity, and voice. And I talk to it like I would talk to a real-life colleague; we were just reviewing the summary it generated from the Zoom transcript of one of our team meetings. I was skeptical at first, but you know I have been complaining about being overwhelmed with administrivia. A friend of mine suggested I experiment with it. So far, so good. It turns out the company has a contract to use a particular AI tool, so I was able to quickly get permission and the security taken care of so the company data is protected. I can't imagine the hurdles I might have faced if they had not already developed a policy. One of our employees was fired earlier this year for using an outside AI tool to summarize project documentation. It was regarded as a security breach because the tool was not owned or licensed by the company and was not run on a company computer but at home."

There was a pause while Tegan looked thoughtful. "Do you use any AI in your coaching practice?" she asked.

The coach was about to answer with complete confidence that she does not. She had not even been tempted to try out any AI tools even when her friends and colleagues were talking enthusiastically about it!

Then, just as she was about to answer, she paused. *How do I know for sure?* she thought.

She began to answer Tegan very carefully. "Well, I haven't taken any of our sessions and plugged them into an AI tool, and I don't record our sessions, so there are no transcripts. I don't even take notes that I could share with an application. I was going to answer with an emphatic 'no.' But I don't know for sure that some of the coaching platforms I use don't integrate some AI. And we are coaching through a third-party arrangement, so their tools may have AI involved. That is a great question.

And one I should know the answer to. I will get back to you about that if that's okay."

---

**I don't think we—as emotional beings—can be replaced by AI. It's an assistant to me for when I need one.**

*—Maravi Melendez-Davis*

---

After the session, the coach began doing her homework. She discovered that one of the coaching tools tracks topics that the coach records as the general session topics and utilizes the trends and recurring themes to suggest resources to the client. The coach was previously unaware of this use of the data and did not have access to the specific resources sent to the client (unless she personally sent them herself).

She also discovered that another coaching program she was part of used AI to match possible coaches to clients. Clients always had the option to choose between multiple coaches, but the AI tool determined which coaches to recommend.

Finally, the coach investigated her coaching accreditation organization to find out their stance on the use of AI. She discovered that they were already quite far along in analyzing the associated risks and opportunities and in making recommendations to coaches and clients on how to consider AI.

Until Tegan asked about AI, the coach had not considered how little she knew about where and how it is already being used.

She started to consider how AI could enhance her coaching and how it might be detrimental. She decided to sign up for some discussion forums and webinars to find out more.

## Evolving Thoughts as Tools Evolve

Since that first meeting with my friends and colleagues, my beliefs have continued to evolve. The question of whether AI will be used in coaching, for example, seems to have been answered. The question now is "How is AI being used in the coaching I do?"

If you coach for one of the bigger online coaching organizations around the world, you are likely already weaving AI into your coaching whether you realize it or not. The theory is that by using AI we accelerate the coaching revolution and can reach more people. AI can help us tailor the experience, enhance resource recommendations, and may even be able to refine the process of matching coach to client.

> In coaching, we are dealing with people, and often using a little psychology in the process. If coaches rely on AI, they could unintentionally be bringing bogus information into their sessions, and potentially do more harm than good.
>
> —*Dr. Joshua Ramirez, CEO, Institute for Neuro & Behavioral Project Management*

## Smart People See Value

I have never been one to follow the crowd, and new technology usually causes me to stick my head in the sand for the first few months. But I realized in that entrepreneurial women's meeting that some of the smartest, most curious, most thoughtful people I know could see value in AI, and I could learn from them.

At the same time, they are not blind to or ignoring risks. My colleagues are adopting a mindset of wary curiosity.

I opened my eyes and ears to join them as they find out more.

## It's Not Whether We Use AI—It's How We Use It. . .

It may be trite to say that many inventions in human history have been seen as devilish and evil only to later become commonplace. Phones, TV, electric lights, they all raised suspicion. Many theories and inventions that we now take for granted resulted in their originators being ostracized, tortured, imprisoned, and even killed.

AI exists. It is likely to be integrated into many aspects of life going forward, including coaching. Generally, I believe the intent will be good, *and* I believe that as always, there will be unintended consequences.

As in all things, some coaches are effective and others less so. Some coaches will integrate AI to really enhance the coaching experience for client and coach alike. Others will use AI poorly, and the result may be that a coach who would previously have had a limited reach may be able to deliver poor coaching to more people going forward. Buyer beware!

The best coaches will think long and hard about how and when to use AI. They will be transparent with their clients. They will consider the ethics of AI-enhanced coaching and follow closely if not get involved in the professional discussions about AI in coaching.

## . . . And How Transparent We Are

To me, more important than how we use AI is how transparent we are about it with our clients and what controls we put in place to ensure the client has the maximum choice and control over their coaching experience.

At all times, we want coaching to be client driven—not coach driven or AI driven. Coaches and their tools, including AI, are here to support the client's journey.

### 10 Questions Coaches Should Ask Themselves

1. Based on what I know now, how important do I believe AI is going to be in providing coaching in the future?
2. How well do I understand what AI does—and does not do?
3. What else do I need to know—and how will I find out?
4. How do the tools I use specifically use AI?
5. What do I need to discuss with my clients about the ways I am experimenting with or using AI in my coaching practice?
6. If a client doesn't want me to use AI in their coaching experience, how will I document that, track that, and demonstrate good faith to the client?
7. In what ways do I believe that AI can enhance my coaching? How do I test those theories?
8. What are 3–5 things I need to keep in mind to ensure that my use of AI in coaching is ethical?
9. What changes will I make in my coaching contracts to protect myself and my clients based on the development of AI tools?
10. How do I stay current with the standards and ethical guidelines of my coaching profession?

### AI Coaching Risks

1. Clients cannot make informed choices because they are unaware of what parts of their coaching experience are human and which are AI driven.
2. Biases in AI programs interfere with the autonomy of the client.

3. Confidentiality is compromised and data is used inappropriately.

4. Coaches rely on AI to the extent that they don't tailor the coaching experience for the client and coaching becomes too generic and not client focused. It becomes like insurance, where coaching is given based on the group of people you belong to—middle-aged, changing careers, empty nester, recently divorced, educated to college level, for example.

5. Coaches put too much trust in the AI models and replace their own experience and good judgment with the advice coming from AI.

6. AI encourages behaviors that are less coaching and more mentoring and consulting. Coaches might start to compromise their roles.

7. Clients put more—or less—trust in the coaching process knowing that it is augmented by AI.

8. AI becomes integrated to the point that it is hard for a client to be sure what is being supplied by AI tools and what the individual coach is adding.

9. Clients are not able to tell when they are—and are not—in contact with a live human coach.

10. Coaching tools are developed to provide feedback that advances a coach's personal, political, or business agenda more than the agenda of the client.

11. Clients have less say in and awareness of how their coaching is being delivered and what models are implicitly being used.

## AI Coaching Opportunities

1. AI can offer the potential for greater consistency across coaches.

2. AI can provide access to coaching resources for more people worldwide.

3. AI can increase the speed of the analysis of client's language, responses, energy, etc.

4. AI can summarize coaching sessions and provide automated notes and feedback for clients.

5. AI can offer coaching mentoring for coaches—a second opinion, if you will.

6. AI can monitor and track key performance metrics for the coach, such as:

a. The proportion of a session spent with the client vs. the coach talking

b. An analysis of repeated themes across sessions

c. The development of a roadmap of progress over many sessions

d. AI-assisted personalized coaching tools and practices

e. Sustainable 24:7 contact with the coach

7. AI can track the trends and averages in sessions, allowing the coach to focus on unique and insightful moments and topics.

---

**Sure, use it as a tool, a starting point to supplement more in-depth research. Meanwhile, come back to me in 10 years when the tech has improved. I may have a different answer!**

**—Dwayne Allen Thomas, Lawyer, Writer & Cookie Connoisseur**

---

# Coaching Is for the Client, Not the Coach

The measures of success of a coaching relationship come from the client. However, research has shown that the best predictor of the success of the coaching process is the relationship between the client and the coach. Exploration of how and whether AI is used in the coaching process is another way to develop rapport.

Coaches and their clients should agree about the use of AI as they explore options, set goals, and plan pathways to development and growth.

And the coach and client will want a plan to adjust their AI expectations as the tools evolve, understanding that new standards will emerge.

In addition to the questions that clients already ask their coaches—and themselves—before engaging a coach, here are 12 new questions that clients might want to explore with their coach.

## 12 Questions for Clients to Ask Their Coach

1. In a word or a short phrase, describe your current view of AI in coaching.

2. Which AI tools are you already using and how do you use them in your coaching practice?

3. If and when that changes, how will you let me know?

4. What say will I have in how you use AI in my coaching experience?

5. If I agree that you can use AI to augment our coaching experience, how will you protect my data?

6. What do you know about current standards on AI use in coaching?

7. What tools do you use for coaching and how do those tools use AI?

8. If I want our coaching to be strictly human-human, is that an option?

9. Who do you consult with to understand the implications of AI in coaching?

10. What is your experience being coached by AI or by a combination of human coach and AI?

11. Who do you use as a mentor or consulting coach?

12. How does (each of) the AI tool(s) you use answer the following question: What are the risks of using AI in coaching?

## What Does AI Think About the Ethics of AI in Coaching?

Since that first meeting with my colleagues, I have been experimenting. I decided to ask a couple of AI tools for their analysis of AI in coaching. My first question was not an open question. I was not yet used to thinking of AI as able to handle open questions.

I started with the following question:

"Is it ethical to use AI in coaching?"

I submitted the question to Bard (the Google tool) and within seconds received the following response:

*Whether or not it is ethical to use AI in coaching is a complex question with no easy answer. There are a number of factors to consider, such as the specific ways in which AI is being used, the potential benefits and risks of using AI, and the ethical guidelines that govern the coaching profession.*

*On the one hand, AI can be used to enhance coaching in a number of ways. For example, AI can be used to:*

■ *Provide clients with personalized feedback and insights based on their individual needs and goals*

- *Help coaches to identify patterns and trends in their clients' behavior that may be difficult to spot on their own*

- *Automate tasks such as scheduling appointments and sending reminders, freeing up coaches to focus on their clients*

*On the other hand, there are also a number of potential risks associated with the use of AI in coaching. For example, there is the risk that AI could be used to manipulate or exploit clients. Additionally, AI could be used to create a "filter bubble" around clients, preventing them from being exposed to new ideas and perspectives.*

*It is important to note that AI is still a relatively new technology, and there is still much that we do not know about its potential impact on coaching. As a result, it is important to use AI in a responsible and ethical way.*

*Here are some ethical considerations to keep in mind when using AI in coaching:*

- *Transparency: Coaches should be transparent with their clients about how they are using AI. Clients should be aware of the ways in which AI is being used to collect, store, and use their data.*

- *Consent: Clients should give their informed consent before their data is used in AI-powered coaching.*

- *Bias: AI systems can be biased, and this bias can be reflected in the results of AI-powered coaching. Coaches should be aware of the potential for bias and take steps to mitigate it.*

- *Privacy: Coaches should take steps to protect the privacy of their clients' data. This includes using secure data storage and encryption, and limiting access to data to only those who need it.*

- *Accountability: Coaches should be accountable for the use of AI in their coaching practice. This means being able to explain how AI is being used, and why certain decisions are being made.*

*Ultimately, the decision of whether or not to use AI in coaching is a personal one. Coaches should carefully weigh the potential benefits and risks before making a decision.*

*Overall, I believe that AI has the potential to be a valuable tool for coaches. However, it is important to use AI in a responsible and ethical way. By following the ethical considerations outlined above, coaches can help to ensure that their clients have a positive and beneficial coaching experience...*[1]

---

[1] Text generated by Bard, Google, September 25, 2023, `https://bard.google.com`

I asked the same question of ChatGPT and received the following answer:

*The ethical use of AI in coaching is a complex and evolving topic. Whether it is ethical to use AI in coaching depends on how AI is employed and the ethical principles and guidelines followed in its implementation. Here are some key points to consider:*

1. *Ethical intentions: The ethicality of using AI in coaching depends on the intentions behind its use. If the goal is to enhance the coaching process, improve outcomes for clients, and uphold ethical standards, then it can be considered ethical.*

2. *Transparency: Coaches should be transparent about the use of AI in coaching interactions. Clients should be aware that AI tools are being used and understand their role in the coaching process.*

3. *Client consent: Clients should provide informed consent for the use of AI in their coaching. They should understand how AI will be used, what data will be collected, and how it will be used to support their coaching journey.*

4. *Human oversight: While AI can provide valuable insights and recommendations, it should not replace human coaches. There should always be human oversight to ensure that the coaching relationship remains at the forefront, and clients have access to human support when needed.*

5. *Bias mitigation: Efforts should be made to mitigate biases in AI algorithms used in coaching. Bias can negatively affect coaching outcomes, so continuous monitoring and adjustments are essential.*

6. *Data privacy and security: Coaches and organizations must prioritize data privacy and security. Client data should be handled with care, in compliance with data protection laws and regulations.*

7. *Client well-being: AI should be used in ways that promote the well-being and personal growth of clients. It should not exploit vulnerabilities or cause harm to clients.*

8. *Professional competence: Coaches should be adequately trained and competent in using AI tools. Continuous professional development is crucial to ensure ethical use of AI.*

9. *Accountability: Coaches and organizations should establish clear lines of accountability for the use of AI in coaching. Coaches should be accountable for the outcomes of coaching sessions, even when AI is involved.*

10. *Feedback and improvement: Clients' feedback about their experiences with AI in coaching should be actively sought and used to improve the coaching process.*

11. *Cultural sensitivity: AI tools used in coaching should be sensitive to cultural differences to ensure inclusivity and avoid causing discomfort or offense to clients from diverse backgrounds.*

    *In summary, the ethical use of AI in coaching is possible when it is implemented with transparency, consent, fairness, and a commitment to the well-being and empowerment of clients. Ethical considerations should guide the development and deployment of AI tools in coaching to ensure that they complement the human coaching relationship and provide value without compromising ethical standards.[2]*

A couple of things stood out to me.

First, not every AI tool provides the same answer to the same question.

The answers I received seemed quite thoughtful and disarmingly responsible.

I wonder what the biases were of the people who coded the AI in the first place.

As AI evolves and presumably moves on from those original biases, will it become "open-minded" or laissez-faire about its use in coaching? (I made a note to ask the same question again in a few months' time!)

How will recommendations from coaching organizations such as the International Coaching Federation (ICF) or the European Mentoring and Coaching Council (EMCC) change the answer to these questions going forward?

## How Do We Deliver the Promise of Coaching Without Tools Such as AI?

In the November 10, 2021, edition of *Frontiers of Psychology*, well-known and well-respected coach Sir Jonathan Passmore coauthored an article with Rosie Evans-Krimme about the future of coaching.[3]

The writers proposed a five-stage model of coaching evolution that suggests we are entering stage four—the time when coaching is going to

---

[2] Text generated by ChatGPT, OpenAI, September 25, 2023, `https://chat.openai.com/chat`

[3] Jonathan Passmore and Rosie Evans-Krimme, "The Future of Coaching: A Conceptual Framework for the Coaching Sector From Personal Craft to Scientific Process and the Implications for Practice and Research," *Frontiers in Psychology* 12:715228 (November 10, 2021): `https://doi.org/10.3389/fpsyg.2021.715228`

become popularized and accessible to more people. This necessitates the use of technology to make that accessibility a reality. During the COVID-19 pandemic, coaches increased their use of virtual conferencing tools to deliver coaching sessions. This means that each coach can potentially reach a wider variety of clients, and clients who previously had no way to experience 1:1 in-person coaching can now access their own coach.

Using technology to tailor the experience is, in Passmore's opinion, a necessary and inevitable step in the progression of coaching.

The use of AI does not mean the end of human coaching. Many aspects of coaching rely on attributes that are yet beyond the capacity of AI, including empathy, emotional intelligence, adaptability based on context, and timing—maybe even some of the ethical questions explored previously in this chapter.

In June of 2023, the *NYU Coaching and Technology Summit* explored this topic further using the Passmore model as a starting point. In their summary of the sessions, NYU graduate students, Pame Barba and Andrea Serbonich identified the following five key takeaways from the summit:[4]

1. *Language*—The use of language is shifting as people make the distinction of "human coach" to differentiate from AI coaches. Panelists agreed that "human" coaching is not going away and is an integral part of the future. Experts agreed that when utilizing technology, it is important to ensure that the human connection and emotional aspect of coaching are not lost.

2. *Coaching mindset*—Attendees were encouraged to remain curious, skeptical, and open-minded about the rapidly moving integration of technology in coaching.

3. *Vigilance*—Experts discussed the importance of governance as AI continues to advance.

4. *Human connection*—The speed at which AI developments are moving toward a more sophisticated, human-like coaching experience is still debatable—some coaching technology companies are claiming a sophisticated and nuanced experience from an AI coach within the next year, whereas others are claiming nothing will ever take the place of a human coach interaction.

5. *Purpose*—Coaching should be focused on helping more people. AI and technology can play a crucial role in achieving this goal.

---

[4] Pame Barba and Andrea Serbonich, "Reflecting on the Potential of AI in Coaching: A Glimpse into the NYU Summit," Global Digital Library - Thought Leadership Institute, August 25, 2023, https://thoughtleadership.org/ reflecting-on-the-potential-of-ai-in-coaching-a-glimpse- into-the-nyu-summit

> I believe there's a place for AI in coaching for administrative activities, time management, and thought-provoking. I'm not ready to replace coaching and the human connection with AI. We are social beings, for now.
>
> —*Dorisse Shakir-Ullah, Career Strategist & Facilitator*

## Case Study: Jamal

Jamal's coach has been researching AI and is interested in using some tools to augment her coaching process. She has some ideas but also wants to make sure that she is thoughtful and ethical and that her clients are part of the process.

She invites Jamal for a discussion about AI in coaching outside their regular coaching sessions. She is not going to charge anything for the session, as she regards it to be similar to the first contract discussions.

As Jamal signs in, the coach prepares.

"Hi, Jamal," she says. "I wanted to meet with you today to talk about artificial intelligence, or AI. I have been researching the use of AI in coaching and am open to doing some experiments to see how AI might enhance your experience. I won't integrate any AI tools without your knowledge and agreement, though. You are the first client I am having this conversation with. What are your thoughts about AI?"

They continue to discuss the topic and the options. Jamal is curious about AI but had not previously considered its use in coaching. He expresses concerns about where his data might end up and that he won't know what is coming from the coach and what has been "generated" by AI. Over the course the next hour, Jamal and his coach identify the following three ways to experiment with AI:

1. The coach will create a transcript of a session and edit it to remove all the references that could identify Jamal. He will review the edited transcript. The coach will then ask an AI tool to analyze the transcript for themes and to suggest follow-up questions.

2. They will engage in a follow-up session in which the coach will clearly identify when she is using questions or ideas suggested by the AI tool.

3. The coach will use an AI tool to suggest resources that Jamal might want to review in relation to the topics of his coaching session.

After completing these steps, they will revisit the use of AI in their ongoing coaching.

They agree that after the experiment, if they do agree to continue using AI, the coaching contract will be amended to ensure that its use is closely defined and that the coach will always make Jamal aware of potential developments. They will build a regular review into the contract so that they can revisit the topic of AI use every few months.

Jamal says he is nervous but curious. The coach says she feels the same way!

# Conclusion

AI is here. Ignoring it empowers it—or at least leaves us vulnerable to it being used in undesirable ways. We want our coaches to be open-minded and curious. And we want tools to work in our favor.

The reality is likely to be that hiccups will occur and mistakes will be made. We might even look back on this moment in time and wish we had made a different choice. At the same time, we have the capacity to cope, to be thoughtful, and to help steer the ethical use of AI to our benefit.

## A Call to Action for Coaches

As coaches, let's learn what AI can do for us and for our clients, and understand the risks.

How will you remain current with what AI is bringing to your coaching tools?

How will you articulate your AI use to your clients?

What choice will you give your clients in how big a part AI plays in their coaching experience?

Get involved in exploring the future of AI and the ethics and standards around its use.

## A Call to Action for Clients

Take charge of your coaching journey and ask the following questions:

What matters to you about how AI is used?

How do you want to engage with AI in coaching?

How does your coach plan to use AI?

How do they know how they are using AI?

What choices do you have?

And ask the following questions of your coach's AI tools:

What are the ethical considerations of AI in coaching?

How is my data protected?

How does my coach know what the tool is doing?

## QUESTIONS TO ASK YOURSELF ABOUT AI

- In a word or a short phrase, what is my current view of AI?
- How do I want AI to be used in my coaching experience? (Do I want to engage in AI-assisted coaching or agree up front that my coaching will be human to human?)
- What do I know about AI that can be used in coaching now?
- If I am using a coaching platform to access coaching, what do I know about how that platform uses AI?
- What do I want to know about how my coach uses AI?
- What do I need to feel safe working with my coach?
- How does my coach's attitude toward AI compare to mine?
- How will I be sure what my coach is providing?
- How important is it that my coach be governed by a set of coaching standards (such as ICF, EMCC, etc.)?
- Who will guide me?

# Core Competencies for Clients

There are several coaching associations around the world. Examples include the International Coaching Federation (ICF) and the European Mentoring and Coaching Council (EMCC). Coaches who are members of those associations are guided by a code of ethics, and their coaching is informed by a set of coaching competencies.

Regardless of the association a coach belongs to, the foundation of all coaching practices is to:

Be ethical

Be self-aware and always learning

Be coaches

Take the lead from the client

Prioritize relationship and environment

Be an advocate for the client

Act in ways that build trust and make the client feel safe

Be fully "in the room" with the client

Coaches who choose to be members of and certified by the International Coaching Federation (ICF) must follow specific guidelines on how to behave (ICF Code of Ethics) and how to coach (ICF Coaching Competencies).

The eight competencies are as follows[1]:

A. **Foundation**
   1. Demonstrates Ethical Practice
   2. Embodies a Coaching Mindset

B. **Co-Creating the Relationship**
   3. Establishes and Maintains Agreements
   4. Cultivates Trust and Safety
   5. Maintains Presence

C. **Communicating Effectively**
   6. Listens Actively
   7. Evokes Awareness

D. **Cultivating Learning and Growth**
   8. Facilitates Client Growth

The EMCC competencies are as follows[2]:

1. Understanding Self
2. Commitment to Self-development
3. Managing the Contract
4. Building the Relationship
5. Enabling Insight and Learning
6. Outcome and Action Orientation
7. Use of Models and Techniques
8. Evaluation

But what about the clients? What guidance are they provided on how to be the best coaching clients that they can be? The answer is, not much. The following are six competency groups that are key to a successful engagement with your coach and the best coaching outcome for you:

1. **Be Prudent and Intentional**
   Do your homework to find the right coach. In Appendix E, I suggest some questions to help you find the right coach for you in the

---

[1] https://coachingfederation.org/app/uploads/2021/03/
ICF-Core-Competencies-updated.pdf
[2] www.emccglobal.org/wp-content/uploads/2018/10/
EMCC-competences-framework-v2-EN.pdf

moment. Not all coaches are alike. They have different styles, lived experiences, work experiences, ages, native languages, customs, and religions. Just as the client arrives as a package (the total of their life and beliefs to date), so does the coach. Accredited coaches have been trained to be aware of and, as far as possible, suspend their biases during coaching sessions. And yet coaches are human too. You want to find a coach that will provide the support you want. And that may mean a different coach for different purposes or at different times on your journey.

1.1 Check out the coach before you meet them. Review their website and LinkedIn profile (and other social media, if applicable), ask for a résumé and credentials, and request testimonials.

1.2 Be ready to interview several coaches to find the right one for you. A good coach will expect this and will not be offended if you choose someone else! A good coach will help you find the right coach for you, even if it is not them.

1.3 Be open to the possibility that your coach may not have direct experience in your role, field, or lifestyle.

1.4 Bring at least a general outline of what you want from coaching. The following are just some of the typical reasons for a client to come to a coach:

To find someone independent to explore options and decisions within a safe environment

To create a plan for achieving a specific learning, career, life or other personal goal (e.g., weight management, fitness)

To explore relationship (personal, professional, or general) challenges and opportunities

To have long-standing beliefs challenged and to explore new perspectives

To consolidate learning

To brainstorm ideas

To identify values and beliefs

To create a sense of purpose and meaning

To explore parenting options

To develop as a leader or manager

2. **Be Hopeful and Persistent**
Even small changes and learnings can make a big difference. Big goals are achieved a step at a time. If you don't believe that, think back to where you were 5 years ago. Would the person you were then believe who you are and what you're doing now?

2.1 Expect to spend time clarifying your visions for the future to make them as clear and concrete as possible.

2.2 Be ready to explore different pathways to your goals—even some that may seem silly or pointless. This is where ideas come from!

2.3 Expect your coach to help you see what you can do to get closer to your goal. The coach will not achieve the goal for you, nor should they tell you what pathway to follow.

2.4 Be clear about how you want your coach to support you and keep you accountable to your plan.

2.5 The coaching relationship develops over time. Trust and safety increase, and the rapport between coach and client builds as they develop a common language specific to them. It is worth the wait!

3. **Be Strong and Vulnerable**
The more we can find out about our strengths, what sets us apart from others, the more pathways we can identify to achieve our purpose.

3.1 Practice seeing the strengths of others—even people who frustrate you—to hone your strengths-spotting capabilities.

3.2 Think about the sailboat metaphor from Dr. Robert Biswas-Diener. Your strengths are the wind in your sails, and your weaknesses and so-called "development opportunities" are the cracks in the hull. Focus on patching the cracks and enhancing the trim of the sails and the wind in your sails!

3.3 Be kind to yourself as you travel on your journey.

3.4 As your confidence in your coach increases, be open to more challenging ideas and questions.

4. **Be Curious and Experimental**
When we bring curiosity and an experimental mindset to a situation, it opens us up to learning new things and taking new approaches to old problems. Every experiment succeeds because it provides useful feedback. If you get the result you wanted and expected, you know what to do going forward. If you don't get the result you wanted and expected, you know what *not* to do going forward!

4.1 When choosing a coach, ask questions to establish whether they are a fit for you. You may want to ask about records, confidentiality, and how the coaching arrangement will work.

Or you may want to focus more on the coach's beliefs and coaching methods.

4.2 During the coaching engagement, bring curiosity to sessions so that you can get the most out of them. Coaches will often challenge your assumptions and gently question your beliefs. Be open to this process so that your beliefs evolve to become more useful to you.

4.3 Check in regularly to make sure you are still getting what you want from coaching. Long-term coaching relationships are great for building trust and safety, but they can become stale, reinforcing, and repetitive. Look out for signs that it is time to engage someone with a different perspective.

5. **Be Brave and Honest**

Coaching is a growth opportunity, and that sometimes means some discomfort along the way. Discomfort is not in itself a bad thing. During coaching, try to adopt an attitude of being comfortable with being uncomfortable. Coaching should challenge and stretch you; it should not undermine you.

5.1 If your coach says something discordant or makes you uncomfortable, let them know, either in the moment or after the session—whenever is more comfortable.

5.2 Let your coach know if they are pushing too hard or asking questions that feel too probing. If working with your coach regularly makes you feel more uncomfortable than feels appropriate, consider changing coaches.

5.3 Your coach is not there to tell you what to do. Be brave about experimenting and be ready to learn from failed experiments!

6. **Be Respectful and Collaborative**

Effective coaches put a lot of thought, practice, and training into their practice and clients. We are your supporters; we think the best of you; we want the best for you—whatever you decide that is. We continue to learn and develop our skills, honing our coaching as we go along. Being a coach is itself a journey, not a destination. We work hard for you.

6.1 Sometimes coaching looks easy, but the coach works hard to listen for things you do and don't say. We listen for changes in cadence, energy, enthusiasm, mood. We listen for times when silence is most useful and times when it makes sense to interrupt a repetitive thought. We are open to any topic, and yet we keep your stated agenda in mind as a reference point, helping you to be intentional about how you spend your time in coaching. During the coaching session, the coach is all about you!

6.2 Expect to work. The most effective coaching relationships are those in which the client is committed, engaged, and ready to do work to make change, analyze options, or develop skills.

6.3 Some topics are not suitable for coaching alone. For example, coaches cannot give legal or financial advice, and they don't teach. Be ready to add to your personal/professional development team with other professionals as you and your coach identify needs.

**Extra Tip!**

Know when to change or stop. Sometimes we need a break; other times we need a different cadence in our coaching.

For example, new clients often initially meet weekly or biweekly, and then, as their needs clarify and their plans solidify (if they are pursuing specific goals), they may go to once a month or even once a quarter. Some clients don't have regular coaching schedules; they arrange a session when they need it.

A successful coaching relationship takes work from the coach and the client, but sometimes the client might not have the bandwidth or energy to do the work. Taking a break is fine!

There may come a time, however much you like your coach, that you feel the need for something different. Effective coaches know this, and their priority is that you have the best coaching experience possible. You may even want to use your existing coach to help you identify what you want in your next coach!

The coaching relationship is a partnership that is 100% focused on you. Be ready for great things!

# Tegan's Profile

| CATEGORY | ROLE/LABEL |
|---|---|
| Race | White |
| Appearance | Green eyes, brown hair, moderate build |
| Gender | Female |
| Sexual preference | LGBTQ |
| Children | 1 adopted girl, at college |
| Primary family roles | Spouse, mother, primary breadwinner |
| Secondary family roles | Sister, daughter, sister-in-law, daughter-in-law |
| Other roles | Friend, colleague |
| Primary language | English, Welsh |
| Mindset | Adventurous, iconoclast, culture-shifter |
| Mental health | Bipolar, managed with medication and exercise |
| Education | College graduate |
| Influencer: spouse | White; first-generation college; grew up as an only child |

*Continues*

*(continued)*

| CATEGORY | ROLE/LABEL |
|---|---|
| Influencer: teacher | School headmistress in high school; independent woman, living alone; no children but passionate about girls' education; educated at state schools but did teacher training programs at several universities in the UK and Europe |
| Influencer: paternal grandparents | No knowledge of paternal family |
| Influencer: maternal grandparents | Grandparents became world travelers after retirement; biggest influence were the postcards and letters Tegan received from them as they traveled; when they died, she inherited their diaries, which told her a lot about their experiences abroad |
| Influencer: sister | Married, two children; family-oriented, driven; lives in Italy |
| Location of upbringing | North Wales; Toronto, Canada |
| Education | Comprehensive school, Wales; Toronto School of Management, Toronto, Canada; University of Bath, England |
| Educational studies | High school (math and science); college (management studies); university (economics) |
| Role models | Mother, who worked and provided for the family; headmistress of high school, who modeled being her own person |
| Anti-role models | Powerful men, national and international politicians, people who use their power to dominate others (e.g., actors, directors, politicians) |
| Passions | Nature, social causes, education, advancing education for girls across the globe, exercise, saying what needs to be said |
| Health | Generally good; used to be very physically active; not much information about family history |
| Socioeconomic status | Lower middle class |
| Living situation | Living in Brazil as a result of a work assignment, which may be her last assignment before retiring; rented home shared with spouse and daughter when she is back from school |
| Living conditions | Developing industrial state; running water, city sewer; moderate level of general comfort, some conveniences; air pollution and crowding; not many open spaces near to home |

# Jamal's Profile

| CATEGORY | ROLE/LABEL |
| --- | --- |
| Race | Asian |
| Appearance | Brown eyes, black hair, moderate build |
| Gender | Male |
| Sexual preference | Heterosexual |
| Children | No children yet but wants them |
| Primary family roles | Son, sibling |
| Secondary family roles | Cousin, brother-in-law, uncle |
| Other roles | Friend, student, colleague |
| Primary language | Hindi, Urdu, English |
| Mindset | Curious, innovative, incubator |
| Mental health | Generally good with occasional short-term mood swings |
| Education | High school, planning to go to university |
| Influencer: mother | Indian; graduate of the Indian Institute of Technology (IIT) Hyderabad, India; retired teacher |

*Continues*

*(continued)*

| CATEGORY | ROLE/LABEL |
|---|---|
| Influencer: father | Indian; also a graduate of IIT Hyderabad; manager in an IT sourcing firm; travels often for work |
| Influencer: paternal grandparents | Neither grandparent went to university but were passionate about learning and education; grandfather worked on the railway; grandmother took care of village children while their parents worked |
| Influencer: maternal grandparents | Mother was adopted and did not know her birth parents; adoptive family owned a store selling food and beverages; education was very important to them, and they worked hard to send all their children (four) to secondary, higher secondary school, and then university |
| Influencer: sister | Married, two children; emigrated to Canada in 2000; graduate of McGill University, Montreal, Canada, where she studied engineering |
| Location of upbringing | Jaipur, India |
| Education | Local primary and secondary school in Jaipur; IIT Hyderabad |
| Educational studies | Math, science |
| Role models | Mother, who became a successful teacher while raising Jamal and his sister; father, for being adventurous and traveling to so many places; sister, for going abroad to school and then staying in Canada |
| Anti-role models | Anyone who appears corrupt or dishonest; anyone who believes that some people are better than others |
| Passions | Nature, learning, sports (especially cricket), movies, music, riding his bike |
| Health | Generally good; very physically active playing school sports; vegetarian diet |
| Socioeconomic status | Lower middle class |
| Living situation | Currently living in his parents' rented apartment in Jaipur; has his own room |
| Living conditions | Developing industrial state; running water, city sewer; moderate level of general comfort, some conveniences; air pollution and crowding; plenty of open spaces; countryside to visit most weekends |

# What to Ask a Potential Coach

The following table includes 20 starter questions to ask when interviewing potential coaches. Take the opportunity to review their website and social media, and then use the interview to check some of the details. These questions apply whether you are considering group (many-to-one) or individual (one-to-one) coaching. In some cases, there are two options for the question. Feel free to use both (or neither).

Without a track record, newly accredited coaches can find getting new clients difficult. This is where other work experience is relevant, as well as the story of how they became a coach. Newer coaches are not bad coaches. Find out what other experience they have. Often new coaches are newly accredited but have been offering coaching as a manager, leader, or HR professional.

Always ask about a free coaching session, to try out the process and to see if you and the coach are a good fit. Both the coach and the client need to feel that the relationship can be productive and supportive. The coach may feel that they cannot provide what you are looking for and recommend a different coach. They want you to have a positive coaching experience, which means finding the right coach for you in this moment. Most coaches will provide the names of other coaches to consider (at least three) or websites and services for finding an alternative.

| SUGGESTED QUESTION | PURPOSE |
|---|---|
| 1. How long have you been coaching? | These questions enable you to get a sense of the coach's level of experience, training, and niche. |
| 2. How did you decide to become a coach? | |
| 3. Who did you train with? | |
| 4. Where did you work before becoming a coach (if applicable)? | |
| 5. Who are your typical clients? | |
| 6. How does your coaching model work?<br><br>or<br><br>How would you describe your approach to coaching? | The specific model is less important than finding out how a coach approaches coaching.<br><br>A key factor in coaching is that it is client-centric. While most coaches will provide guidance and ideas, beware of coaches who have a set agenda, predefined coaching topics, or a program. |
| 7. If you were looking for a coach, what would you ask them? | This question enables you to find out what the coach believes is important to know, which provides insight into the coach's style and possible biases. |
| 8. What is helpful for me to know about you? | Coaches should generally be willing to be vulnerable without providing too much detail. The answer to this question often provides insight into who the coach is and what the relationship is likely to be like. |
| 9. What do you need to know about me? | Coaches generally want to know what brings you to coaching and how the success of the coaching engagement will be measured. They may ask about your values or your biggest obstacles. Effective coaches are curious. |
| 10. How many clients do you see every day/week?<br><br>or<br><br>How do you get ready for a coaching session? | A coach's effectiveness can vary based on the number of clients they see every day or week. Consider carefully how effective a coach is likely to be after 5–6 clients in a day or 15 clients in a week. |

*Continues*

*(continued)*

| SUGGESTED QUESTION | PURPOSE |
| --- | --- |
| 11. What is your record retention policy? | Client information is confidential, but it is not protected by legal privilege (as with an attorney or clergyperson). Your coach should ensure you that only minimum information will be stored and that it will be deleted or destroyed once the engagement is over. |
| 12. How do you protect confidentiality? | Look for secure recordkeeping and no sharing of personal details. The coach will generally suggest that sessions be in a quiet private place and not use workplace accounts and equipment. |
| 13. What determines whether coaching is successful? | Coaches will often mention your commitment and hard work. Rapport is another key factor, building trust and creating a safe environment. The coach will probably also ask you what is most important in helping you to feel safe. |
| 14. How often do you receive coaching? | Coaches are recommended to be coached themselves. It is important to experience the process from the clients' perspective *and* that coaches practice what they preach. Coaches may be in a mentor group, under supervision, or working with their own coach. |
| 15. What are your favorite topics for coaching? | This question allows you to see how a coach's interests align with your reason for coming to coaching. |
| 16. What experience do you have coaching people who want _____? | This is an opportunity to find out whether a coach is experienced and comfortable coaching you for your purpose. |
| 17. What questions should I be asking? | An effective coach will help you make sure you have asked questions that are helpful and that you are as fully informed as possible in making your choice. |

*Continues*

*(continued)*

| SUGGESTED QUESTION | PURPOSE |
|---|---|
| 18. How will I know that coaching is working? | An effective coach will explore with you how *you* will decide whether the coaching is working. This is a client-centric service, and only the client is able to determine the effectiveness. The coach may work with you to brainstorm ways of measuring success. But a coach should not make promises as to outcome, nor should the coach dictate how to measure success. |
| 19. How will I know when it is time to change coaches or stop coaching? | Coaches want their clients to have a good experience. Once a client starts to feel it is time for a change or that the coaching is not as effective over several sessions as it has been in the past, it may be time to reset. Your coach may also recommend other forms of support if it seems that your situation would benefit from a different skill set. |
| 20. What do you recommend as a minimum engagement?<br><br>*or*<br><br>What if I want to cancel before then? | Coaches know that it takes time to build rapport and develop trust, so it is customary to recommend at least three sessions. However, you should always be able to cancel the engagement if you choose to. |

# Is It Time for a Change? Is This a Coaching Moment for You?

Not everything in life is well-suited for coaching. Learning a specific set of skills, for example, is not generally something to be learned by experimentation. Doctors are taught by the see one, do one, teach one method, for example. They are not invited to try one, try another one, and then get some coaching!

So how do you know if something is a coachable topic?

There are no hard and fast rules, but there are some general guidelines that can help. Your coach can also help you determine if your topic is a coachable topic.

What brings you to coaching?

The following answers align with the coaching approach (choose any or even all):

1. Generating ideas and brainstorming, identifying options about the present and future

2. Having a caring but neutral person with whom to discuss plans, options, and decisions, and who is not too close to the situation

3. Planning for change—e.g., a new job, a move, a change in life status

4. Choosing between multiple options in personal or professional life—e.g., the best school to go to, which job to accept

5. Exploring whether change is a good idea at this time

6. Challenging beliefs and assumptions

7. Looking at something from someone else's perspective

8. Setting priorities

9. Being a thought partner

10. Being an accountability buddy

And the following answers suggest that a different professional is likely to be appropriate:

1. Seeking the root cause of some problem in a relationship or job

2. Analyzing the past (coaches often ask clients to mine their past, but only for things they have learned that are useful going forward)

3. Connecting past experiences with current experiences to explain learned behaviors and habits

4. Receiving financial, legal, or other professional advice (although a coach can often help you decide which professional to work with)

5. Dealing with addiction problems

6. Addressing anything likely to require a diagnosis

Note that some other professionals are happy to work with your coach, and some coaches collaborate with other professionals so that you can combine the benefits of different helping professions.

## How Often and How Long?

There is no one-size-fits-all in coaching. You and your coach will work together to come up with a coaching plan that works best for you. Effective coaching is planned but flexible. Your focus and attention are as important as the coach's, and it is important to build a coaching schedule that is as easy as possible to sustain. Consider how different time zones, the working days/hours of you and your coach, any regular travel requirements, etc. may affect your coaching schedule.

Many coaches offer fixed-length sessions, often 30, 45, 60, or 90 minutes. However, coaching is about the value you receive, not the number of minutes. I have had clients who felt complete and that the current coaching session was worthwhile after a session of 15 minutes. Other times I have continued for a full 90 or 120 minutes with an individual because they were still getting use out of the session and we were both available to continue.

Group coaching options tend to be 60 or 90 minutes to ensure that participants have sufficient opportunity to benefit. When considering group coaching, you should check the ratio of coaches to clients. Ideally, groups should be no more than 6–8 people, although with multiple coaches, the cohort may be larger.

As mentioned previously, it is common for coaching programs to have a minimum commitment so that you and your coach have sufficient chance to establish the working relationship and build trust. It is rare that coaching is one and done if you haven't previously worked with the coach.

Lastly, many clients come for coaching on multiple topics. Often they are at different stages of readiness for each. An adaptable coach and a committed client will be flexible.

## Readiness for Change

Even if you have decided a change is needed and you believe coaching is for you, it is helpful to start by exploring your readiness to change. Just because we want change does not mean we are always ready to do the work to make it happen.

As shown in the following table, the five-stage transtheoretical change model[1] is a good way to determine whether now is the time for coaching.

---

[1] DiClemente, C. C., & Prochaska, J. O. (1998). Toward a comprehensive, transtheoretical model of change: Stages of change and addictive behaviors. In W. R. Miller & N. Heather (Eds.), *Treating addictive behaviors* (pp. 3–24). Plenum Press. https://doi.org/10.1007/978-1-4899-1934-2_1. Recovered June 20, 2023: https://psycnet.apa.org/record/1998-06419-001

This diagram represents the change process for most individuals.

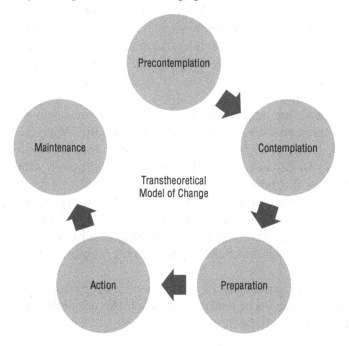

This table explores what the stages look like with a coach.

| CHANGE STAGE | COACH'S ROLE |
| --- | --- |
| **Precontemplation**—You have not even thought about making a change. | This is when you may be sent for coaching—e.g., by your employer to tackle an issue that you have not yet recognized as requiring action. The coach can help you explore whether there is a problem, what the problem is, what change you might want to consider, and where you are in the change process. This may be a single meeting to explore options. |
| **Contemplation**—You are considering a change, identifying the benefits, and assessing the challenges. | You may have been offered coaching or decided to explore coaching yourself because you are thinking about a change. The coach can help you assess your readiness and motivation to change and whether now is the time for change. This may take one or more sessions to help you determine the priority of this change and how committed you are to making the change. |

*Continues*

*(continued)*

| CHANGE STAGE | COACH'S ROLE |
|---|---|
| **Preparation**—You are putting the pieces in place, assessing which resources you have and which additional resources you need. You are planning for change. | Your coach will work with you to put a plan in place for you to follow. Your coach will partner with you to assess which resources you have and which resources you need, and to determine pathways to success. Your coach will help you identify your strengths, what might get in your way, and whose help you need. This is the Hope Building and Strength Identification phase. This may take several sessions meeting weekly or biweekly. |
| **Action**—You are taking steps to make changes or putting your plan into action. | Your coach will help you stay the course, follow the plan, and adjust it as you go. This is the Brave and Curious phase of coaching during which you may have to experience some discomfort to accomplish what you want. Your coach will help you stay accountable and adjust the plan if it does not suit you. They will encourage you to experiment and use success and setbacks as learning opportunities. Coaching sessions will tend to be regular but not as frequent as during the preparation stage. At this stage, you may meet once or twice a month or on an ad hoc/as-needed basis. |
| **Maintenance**—You are continuing along your new path, maintaining new behaviors and habits and recovering from setbacks and "wobbles." | Your coach is often most useful for regular check-ins for accountability. If you slip up in your goals or have a "wobble," your coach can help you look at the situation a different way, challenge assumptions, and offer a different perspective to help you get back on track. Coaching sessions are often more spread out (monthly, quarterly, or as needed). |

# Are *You* Ready for Coaching?

Consider the following questions as you think about support options. Whether you focus on coaching or use coaching in combination with other support professionals, it helps to consider these questions before your first meeting. Coaching is a great support and a wonderful experience, and it can lead to amazing outcomes—as long as you are really ready.

Do you want advice or a teacher? Or, do you want to explore options and make your own plan?

How coachable is your topic?

Are you ready for coaching?

What do you need to be ready for coaching?

# Acknowledgments

As a person who likes to gather a lot of different perspectives, one of the hardest things for me to do when I write is to create the acknowledgments section. There are so many people from whom I draw insights and inspiration, and I am always worrying that I will miss someone important.

There is no way to avoid mistakes and omissions, so the first thing I want to say is THANK YOU, everyone.

If we have crossed paths, there is some part of you and your insights in this book. Maybe you inspired me to look at things in a new way. Maybe you introduced me to a new fact. Maybe you shared something that helped clarify a behavior I want to dial back or avoid. If we have had a conversation, in person, on a call, on a panel, in a class, by email, on social media, THANK YOU. You have contributed!

One group of people I really want to acknowledge is the team at the VIA Institute on Character. They have helped me to hone my writing and presenting skills, have helped me to develop a deep understanding and appreciation of character strengths, and offered a great launchpad for me to become a speaker, author, and coach. Thank you to Dr. Ryan Niemiec, Breta Cooper, Christina Jenkins, and all the team at the Institute—old and new!

I also want to thank all the managers I have worked with over the years and the teams too. They have tolerated and even embraced some of my experiments in team building and communication and have contributed hugely to my understanding of people and my style of coaching and engaging with an audience. From the manager in the UK who made me realize that preparation *is* part of the project (just as agenda building is part of the coaching session) to the leader who first stood me up in front of an audience and told me to "present the project to the audience." From my manager who first called me "Red" to the leader who showed me what "the buck stops here" really means. From the manager who shouted a damning review of my work across the shared workspace to the leaders who decided that I was burned out (they were not wrong) and that it was time for a reshuffle. You all taught me a great deal, and I am enormously thankful!

Of course, there are some people I feel compelled to name specifically and about whom I want to share more information because I want everyone else to know them and what they bring to the table.

The amazing group of women in my entrepreneurial women's group have inspired me to try new things, to reach higher and further, and to acknowledge my doubts and uncertainties and move forward anyway. This group is made up of eight wonderful women who are full of spirit, adventure, and kindness. They are:

Crystal Richards of MindsparQ® launched our PM Collective and is a renowned PMP preparation trainer, and she makes #projectmanagement fun! She is also the creator of the Indoor Recess Summit.

Christina Heath, founder of MangoFlow Consulting is a Strategic Alignment Coach.

Dawn Mahan, founder of PMOtraining.com, was brave enough to record a coaching session with me LIVE so that other PMs can discover the benefits of coaching.

Helen Vavougios is the Principal Consultant of Githio Consulting. She is a shining example of project management in fields ranging from construction to mining and resources to healthcare, and is the Queen of large projects!

Lisa Nelson, founder of See In Colors, is a visual strategist. Her amazing e-book *Let's Draw It Out - Awesome Icons for Visual Thinking* even showed me how to draw out my thoughts and ideas.

Megan Young Gamble is the Project ExecutionHER at Get Level Consulting. Her specialty is packaging in the health and wellness industry.

Tamara McLemore is a project manager trainer and describes herself as an "accidental project manager." Well, the result of that accident is that many project managers are more skilled, more effective, and more confident today after working with Tamara.

Trinesha Longley works as a project manager for large companies, but she left her mark on me when I saw her speak at the 2022 International Institute for Learning IPM Day. She showed me a better way of engaging the audience!

Then there are the amazing people who worked alongside me to develop In It Together Coaching. This remarkable group helped me hone my coaching skills and created a wonderful group coaching program. This book would not be possible without them. They are: Alan Elmore, Angela Carter-Lanon, Brigid Carney, Delia Haydn, Kari Kelly, Mara Salz, Naomi Clark-Turner, Pam McRae, Renée Hutcherson-Lucier, Sylvia Rodriguez, Teresa Schmitz, Tiffine Johnson Davis Good, and Tina Scott-Morgan.

And of course thank you to Jeffrey Sklar who agreed to share his elephant drawings for the section breaks!!

And no acknowledgment would be complete without talking about my business collaborators, Allison Jarrett and Irene Poku. Allison, who retired from the U.S. Air Force to become a coach and trainer, is an expert in resilience—not just teaching it but living it! Irene Poku is a coach in the UK and runs her own coaching company, Paradigm Shift Coaching. She has a wealth of professional and personal experience that helps her to coach clients who want to really discover their authentic selves. I have learned so much from these women and am inspired by them every day, and I cannot wait to see how our collaboration develops in the coming months and years.

Then, of course, there is the team at Wiley Publishing. This book would not have happened if Kenyon Brown had not contacted me and suggested a book exploring coaching—not as a book for coaches about being a better coach but as a book for people curious about what coaching can do for them. Having coached me through the process of getting the book selected, Kenyon put me in touch with the amazing team who designed the book cover, edited my content, vetted my references, designed the interior layout, and made the book available to the world. In particular, I want to thank my editor and project manager, Krysta Winsheimer.

I also want to acknowledge my friends around the world. My friends are great cheerleaders *and* are always willing to challenge my thinking. Some want to remain anonymous; others have already been named above, but to my entire network, I want to say THANK YOU from the bottom of my heart.

And then there is my family. My husband has been endlessly patient—with me, the book, and the twists and turns of my career. He is always a supporter even when he is giving constructive feedback! My son and daughter, Ben and Beckie, and my grandson, Desi, you inspire me to go further!

And to my family in the UK, my sister, Jo, my brother-in-law, Peter (aka PJ), my nephew, John Mark (aka JM), and my nieces, Susannah and Esmé, it has been an adventure, hasn't it? Looking forward to seeing what comes next!

And, finally, to my parents, Rick Kelly and Edna Kelly (née Patient). They messed me up and set me straight in equal measure. The perfect balance.

# About the Author

**Ruth S. Pearce, JD, ACC, CIC, PMP**, is a coach, author, mentor, LinkedIn Learning instructor, and advocate for living life to the fullest. She is passionate about helping us all to break free from self-imposed limitations and craft a life that is meaningful, vibrant, and uniquely ours!

Ruth believes in the power of coaching to help individuals and groups transform their lives, behavior, and relationships, and she is committed to helping her clients get out of their own way and create a life that is truly fulfilling. She also believes that you can get a long way on your own with the right tools!

Ruth has had the privilege of coaching and training countless individuals and groups on their journeys to self-discovery and personal growth. She approaches her work with enthusiasm, guided by her unwavering belief in the boundless potential within each of us. For Ruth, coaching is not just a profession; it is a calling and is a commitment to continuous learning and skill development.

Away from her coaching, speaking, and writing endeavors, Ruth finds relaxation in the pages of a good book. Reading has been her sanctuary, a realm where imagination knows no bounds. She believes that words are not just letters strung together; they are magic, a portal to new worlds and endless possibilities. Books have been Ruth's mentors, teaching her empathy, resilience, and the art of storytelling.

But Ruth is not all about quiet contemplation. You might spot her in the nearby park, indulging in a few cartwheels or dancing with her husband. She believes that age is just a number and the spirit can remain forever young. Laughter is her secret sauce, and playfulness is the thread that weaves through the tapestry of her life.

Ruth's philosophy is straightforward: Life is too short to be anything but intentional. She firmly believes that life satisfaction and legacy are not destinations but ways of life. It's the curiosity that propels us to explore, the courage that enables us to take risks, and the kindness that connects us with others.

After growing up in the UK, Ruth moved to the U.S. in 1995 and became a naturalized citizen. She has lived in New York City, upstate New York, and Western Massachusetts (as far from Boston as you can be and still in the state of Massachusetts). In 2018, she and her husband moved to Durham, North Carolina, and in 2021 to Southport, North Carolina, to enjoy the water and the wildlife. She now lives with her husband Gareth in Chapel Hill, where they share their house with two German Shepherd-Poodle mix dogs, Luka and Misha, and the two Lionhead rabbits that live in Ruth's office, BunnyPenny and Dylan. A daily routine is ensuring that the dogs and the rabbits don't meet. On the rare occasion that they have, a rollicking live game of Whac-A-Mole has ensued. The dogs love it, the rabbits not so much!

In peace & gratitude,

Have thoughts, comments, or questions? Email me at RuthPearce@ ALLELLC.org.

# About the Book
# Advisory Board

When I accepted the opportunity to write this book, one of my stipulations was that I wanted to bring in the perspectives and voices of many people. I am one coach and one person with a certain experience of life. While I am always *full* of ideas, I don't have all the answers, and I learn new things every day. The voices in this book are those who have influenced me and challenged me the most and who have helped me reach the point where this book is even conceivable.

**Todd B. Kashdan, PhD,** is Professor of Psychology at George Mason University and a leading authority on well-being, psychological flexibility, curiosity, courage, and resilience. He has published over 250 peer-reviewed articles, and his work has been cited over 45,000 times. He received the Distinguished Faculty Member of the Year Award from George Mason University and Distinguished Scientific Award for Early Career Contributions from the American Psychological Association. He is the author of *Curious?* and *The Upside of Your Dark Side,* and *The Art of Insubordination: How to Dissent and Defy Effectively.* His writing has appeared in the *Harvard Business Review, the New York Times, National Geographic,* and *Fast Company,* among other publications, and his research is featured regularly in media outlets such as *The Atlantic, the New York Times, NPR,* and *Time magazine.* He's a twin with twin daughters (plus one more), with plans to rapidly populate the world with great conversationalists.

**Dwayne Allen Thomas** is a lawyer, writer, professional napper, and cookie connoisseur. *Psychology Today* promoted his articles *Choosing Death Over Life, How to Beat Any Test*, and *You vs. Your Mentor* to Essential Topics, and his article *On Being an Ally* to an Essential Read. His essay *A White Man Called Me N******* was a semi-finalist in *Boulevard's* Contest for Emerging Writers. Dwayne earned his JD from Brooklyn Law School and a Master of Applied Positive Psychology from the University of Pennsylvania, where he also served as an assistant instructor in its Applied Positive Psychology Certificate Program.

**Julianne Wolfe** is a certified PMP and a seasoned PPM professional with roots in analytical chemistry, laboratory management, and criminal forensics. She focused her early career in the laboratory and discovered the tenets of project management while exploring better ways to lead large research projects. Since then, Julianne has focused on project, program, and portfolio management in various industries, different disciplines, and in diverse initiatives including large-scale global transformations. Through these experiences, she has become an expert in essential skills (aka soft skills, power skills) and is a passionate leader in helping others to hone this skill set.

**Dana Brownlee** is president of Professionalism Matters, an Atlanta-based corporate training firm, a LinkedIn Learning instructor, and former Forbes Careers Senior Contributor. Her book *The Unwritten Rules of Managing Up: Project Management Techniques from the Trenches* was published in February 2019. She has presented at Project Management Institute events throughout the United States and in Costa Rica, Marseille, Milan, and Berlin.

**Dorisse Shakir-Ullah** is a retired Federal Government leader, career coach, mentor, and facilitator. She started Career Forward Coaching, LLC, to empower those in the public and private sectors to grow professionally and personally. Dorisse is editor in chief of the Friends of Government Coaching Review and a member of the Academy of Government and Military Coaching, LLC online coach education team. While volunteering for nonprofits, Dorisse offers women, young adults, and pro-aging communities career essentials, leadership, digital literacy, and coping skills. Her favorite Dr. Martin Luther King Jr. quote, "Life's most persistent and urgent question is, 'What are you doing for others?'" sums up Dorisse's "why" as a volunteer, coach, and mentor. That question inspires her to serve and make a difference.

**Maravi Melendez-Davis, ACC, SHRM-CP, M.Ed.**, works as a catalyst for project success, fostering both leadership and organizational growth. As a project management consultant, learning facilitator and leadership coach, she excels in tailoring solutions to meet specific needs of each client/organization, recognizing that a one-size-fits-all approach is insufficient in dynamic environments. Maravi also specializes in people development and behavioral intelligence, empowering leaders and teams to effectively handle change and show up well through transitions. She is a coleader for the International Coaching Federation's (ICF) Ethics Community of Practice and broadly encourages work-life alignment as a RYT 200 yoga instructor.

**Geoff Crane**, from his career in academia to his time in investment banking, is a true Renaissance man with a message for the world: You can thrive as a life coach, and there are tools that make it possible. His career has spanned multiple countries on several continents, and he has inspired thousands thanks to his endless curiosity and energy.

**Sarbjeet Singh** works as a marketing manager with a liquor startup in Canada. In the past, he has worked as a copywriter and created creative concepts for many prominent brands. Sarbjeet began his career as a database programmer and has experience working for global financial institutions.

**Marjorie Aunos, PhD**, is a psychologist, researcher, speaker, and consultant on accessibility and inclusion. She teaches organizations and educators to solution-find and build environments that are accessible, inclusive, and welcoming to young families with disabilities. Marjorie is the author of *The Power of Purpose for a Parent With Paraplegia* and contributing author to *We've Got This: Essays By Disabled Parents*. Her TEDx talk "What we can learn from disabled parents" has over 200,000 views.

**Demetra Moore** is a leadership development coach with a passion for helping leaders reach their highest potential. This is a love she discovered over a decade ago while working as a mutual fund trader for a Fortune 500 company. Demetra, who always had a desire to be an entrepreneur, made the choice to explore opportunities and started her firm Moore Out of Life. Today, Demetra coaches and trains full-time for Moore Out of Life and partners with Duke Corporate Education as a leadership coach for some of the top organizations in the world. Demetra is also the author of three books and has been featured by multiple news outlets, including *Connected Woman Magazine, the Huffington Post, Black Enterprise, Enterprising Women,* and *Wealth Palace.*

**Kari Kelly** is an Enterprise Agile Coach at Dandy People in Stockholm, Sweden. Her passion is bridging the gap between people and tech so that organizations can thrive in this new paradigm of work, which includes advocating for people in tech with autism. She's worked in an array of industries such as nonprofit, insurance, biopharma, brewing, and technology, the most notable being Apple Retail.

**Renata Rangel, MSc** is a career and well-being consultant and coach, and a doctoral candidate in psychology. She devotes her career to understanding and optimizing human development. Specializing in positive psychology, her research focuses on the relationship between the use of character strengths and engagement and well-being in the workplace. Her deep understanding of human resilience was profoundly enriched following a breast cancer diagnosis in 2022, making her even more committed to helping others unlock their potential and flourish in their lives. Renata is part of a growing network of amazing positive psychology practitioners in Brazil.

**Asila Calhoun** is a certified coach and facilitator whose coaching and consulting business focuses on partnering with leaders through coaching, leadership development, and diversity, equity, and inclusion training. Asila partnered with another coach and consultant to create THRIVVE: Transforming Hurt and Racial Inequities into Vision, Value & Empowerment to support Black women in the workplace. Through their monthly webinars for professional and personal development, they have created a community for Black women to thrive.

**Josh Ramirez** is redefining project management through science! He believes we must have a total paradigm shift in the field of project management, formally recognizing the human factor in the management of projects, and integrating those changes throughout all phases, knowledge areas, and processes. We must pursue formal recognition in the private sector and the public sector, throughout all industries, and throughout all federal organizations, with a top-down change in the way we view and manage projects. They have done it with behavioral economics, behavioral finance, behavioral operations, and behavioral supply chain management. Now, it's project management's turn. He firmly believes this is the next frontier in our discipline: behavioral project management. This is his research, and this is his objective.

**Ozge Ayen Caner** is originally from Turkey, where she was a successful attorney. After deciding with her husband to move to Canada, she has been creating a new life in this new location. Moving to another country is one of the biggest challenges we can face. Navigating a new professional environment, building a new network, and learning the ways of your new home take time and energy. Ozge is a great example of transition done well and with self-compassion.

**Sabra Fowler** is an experienced manager with a successful history of working in the financial services industry. Her wide-ranging skills in sales, account management, leadership, process and risk management, and finance mean that she is versatile and quick to adapt. Sabra is the consummate professional and also a lifelong learner. She embraces every opportunity to develop and learn!

**Sarah Schütte, Solicitor-Advocate and Director, LLB (Hons) CIArb CAPM**: With 20 years' qualified legal experience in London, UK advising on construction, engineering, and infrastructure projects, Sarah aligns contracts with business strategy and desired benefits, advocates confident and competent contract management, and encourages the purposive application of law. She has a specialist practice in project management and is a trainer, facilitator, and mentor. She founded Schutte Consulting Limited in 2014 after working in private practice and as senior in-house counsel for both buyer and vendor. Her tripartite experience makes her a well-rounded problem-solver and considerate adviser with (muddy) boots firmly on the ground! Sarah is focusing on studies for her PMI PMP and to become a CEDR UK accredited mediator. She plans to start 2024 with both of these under her belt!

**Dianne L. McMillan** is an Information Technology (IT) Project Management leader with more than 15 years of experience supporting pharmaceutical, technology, financial services, and e-commerce sectors. Her expertise includes content management systems (CMS), digital transformation, multi-channel marketing, B2B, SaaS, issue resolution, and continuous improvement. She is known for leading collaborative teams to optimize marketing and technology results and effectively communicating with stakeholders to support data-driven decisions.

**Jana Wardian, PhD, MSW**, is on the faculty at the University of Nebraska Medical Center (UNMC) working with hospital physicians designing projects that improve patient care, and is an Associate Director with the Interprofessional Academy of Educators supporting health professions educators preparing UNMC students for the future. She previously served as the Research Director at the Air Force Diabetes Center of Excellence at Lackland AFB in San Antonio, TX from 2015 to 2020. Her passion is seeing others do things they want to do but may not think that they can. No one does anything meaningful on their own.

# Index